CD DISC.

History
Modern World History
Complete Revision and Practice

Allan Todd

Published by BBC Active, an imprint of Educational Publishers LLP, part of the Pearson Education Group Edinburgh Gate, Harlow, Essex CN20 2JE, England

BBC logo © BBC 1996. BBC and BBC Active are trademarks of the British Broadcasting Corporation

First published 2002; revised edition 2010
Third impression 2011

ISBN 978-1-4066-5442-4

Printed in China CTPSC/03

Minimum recommended system requirements
PC: Windows(r), XP sp2, Pentium 4 1 GHz processor (2 GHz for Vista), 512 MB of RAM (1 GB for Windows Vista), 1 GB of free hard disk space, CD-ROM drive 16x, 16 bit colour monitor set at 1024 x 768 pixels resolution
MAC: Mac OS X 10.3.9 or higher, G4 processor at 1 GHz or faster, 512 MB RAM, 1 GB free space (or 10% of drive capacity, whichever is higher), Microsoft Internet Explorer® 6.1 SP2 or Macintosh Safari™ 1.3, Adobe Flash® Player 9 or higher, Adobe Reader® 7 or higher, Headphones recommended

If you experiencing difficulty in launching the enclosed CD-ROM, or in accessing content, please review the following notes:
1 Ensure your computer meets the minimum requirements. Faster machines will improve performance.
2 If the CD does not automatically open, Windows users should open 'My Computer', double-click on the CD icon, then the file named 'launcher.exe'. Macintosh users should double-click on the CD icon, then 'launcher.osx'
Please note: the eDesktop Revision Planner is provided as-is and cannot be supported.
For other technical support, visit the following address for articles which may help resolve your issues:
http://centraal.uk.knowledgebox.com/kbase/

If you cannot find information which helps you to resolve your particular issue, please email: Digital.Support@pearson.com.
Please include the following information in your mail:
- Your name and daytime telephone number.
- ISBN of the product (found on the packaging.)
- Details of the problem you are experiencing - e.g. how to reproduce the problem, any error messages etc.
- Details of your computer (operating system, RAM, processor type and speed if known.)

Contents

* Only available in the CD-ROM version of the book.

Exam board specification map

Provides a quick and easy overview of the topics you need to study for the examinations you will be taking.

* *Covered in your coursework*

Introduction

How to use GCSE Bitesize Complete Revision and Practice

Begin with the CD-ROM. There are five easy steps to using the CD-ROM – and to creating your own personal revision programme. Follow these steps and you'll be fully prepared for the exam without wasting time on areas you already know.

Topic checker

Step 1: Check

The Topic checker will help you figure out what you know – and what you need to revise.

Revision planner

Step 2: Plan

When you know which topics you need to revise, enter them into the handy Revision planner. You'll get a daily reminder to make sure you're on track.

Revise

Step 3: Revise

From the Topic checker, you can go straight to the topic pages that contain all the facts you need to know.

Web Bite

- Give yourself the edge with the Web*Bite* buttons. These link directly to the relevant section on the BBC Bitesize Revision website.

Audio Bite

- Audio*Bite* buttons let you listen to more about the topic to boost your knowledge even further.*

Step 4: Practise

Check your understanding by answering the Practice questions.
Click on each question to see the correct answer.

Exam Bite

Step 5: Exam

Are you ready for the exam? Exam*Bite* buttons take you to an exam question on the topics you've just revised.*

* Not all subjects contain these features, depending on their exam requirements.

Use this book whenever you prefer to work away from your computer. It consists of two main parts:

1 A set of double-page spreads, covering the essential topics for revision from each area of the curriculum. Each topic is organised in the following way:

- a summary of the main points and an introduction to the topic
- lettered section boxes covering the important areas within each topic
- key facts highlighting essential information in a section or providing tips on answering exam questions
- practice questions at the end of each topic to check your understanding.

2 A number of special sections to help you consolidate your revision and get a feel for how exam questions are structured and marked. These extra sections will help you to check your progress and be confident that you know your stuff. They include:

- Topic checker – quick questions covering all topic areas
- exam-style questions and worked model answers and comments to help you get full marks
- Complete the facts – check that you have the most important facts at your fingertips
- Last-minute learner – the most important facts in just in a few pages.

About your exam

Get organised
You need to know when your exams are before you make your revision plan. Check the dates, times and locations of your exams with your teacher, tutor or school office.

On the day
Aim to arrive in plenty of time, with everything you need: several pens, pencils and a ruler.

On your way, or while you're waiting, read through your Last-minute learner.

In the exam room
When you are issued with your exam paper, you must not open it immediately. There are, however, some details on the front cover that you can fill in before you start the exam itself (your name, centre number, etc.). If you're not sure where to write these details, ask one of the invigilators (teachers supervising the exam).

When it's time to begin writing, read each question carefully. Remember to keep an eye on the time.

Finally, don't panic! If you have followed your teacher's advice and the suggestions in this book, you will be well prepared for any question in your exam.

Long-term causes

 With the creation of the new state of Germany in 1871, tensions in Europe between the Great Powers increased.

 The main areas that led to rivalry were industrial competition, the gaining of colonies and a growing arms race.

 These tensions led to the creation of two rival Alliance systems.

A Economic and colonial rivalry

>> **key fact** By 1900, colonies were very important to European nations – for cheap raw materials to expand industry, for export markets and as military bases.

- After 1888, the new **Kaiser** of Germany, Wilhelm II, wanted Germany to have colonies, especially in Africa and Asia. This led to opposition from Britain and France – the two main rival imperial powers.

- These tensions with Germany over colonies led Britain and France to sign the **Entente Cordiale in 1904**.

- The Kaiser tested this new agreement in what became known as the **First Moroccan Crisis in 1905**. This actually drove Britain and France closer together (France wanted Morocco as a colony).

- Six years later, there was a second, more serious Moroccan crisis – the **Agadir Crisis of 1911**. Again, Britain and France stood together, and Germany had to back down and accept land in the French Congo. However, tensions had risen even further.

- Britain was also concerned about **Germany's expanding industry**, which in more modern areas (e.g. electrical, chemicals and steel) began to leave Britain behind.

> **remember >>**
> The Entente Cordiale, which means 'friendly understanding', was not an agreement to support each other in war.

> **remember >>**
> A country's economic and industrial strength affected the size and strength of its armed forces.

B The arms race

>> **key fact** Throughout the nineteenth century, Britain's navy had been the strongest in the world. By 1890, the growth of trade and the expansion of empire made control of the seas even more important.

- However, from 1898, the new Kaiser of Germany announced plans to greatly expand the new German navy. From 1906, Britain responded by building bigger battleships known as **dreadnoughts**. Soon, a naval arms race developed between Britain and Germany.

> **remember >>**
> In the Franco-Prussian War of 1870–1, Prussia defeated France. Prussia then became the main part of a new German nation. France was forced to pay compensation and give the provinces of Alsace and Lorraine to this new Germany.

- At the same time, many other countries began building up their armies, especially France, Russia and Germany – these all introduced **conscription**. By 1914, there were five million soldiers in the combined armies of the Great Powers.

- In addition, as tensions increased, all countries began drawing up plans for war (e.g. Germany's **Schlieffen Plan** and France's **Plan XVII**).

C The Alliance System

>> **key fact** The emergence of Germany after 1871 as a new Great Power led to the countries of Europe dividing themselves into two separate and rival alliances.

- In the 1880s, the new Germany tried to keep France isolated so that it would not easily be able to attack to recover Alsace–Lorraine. By 1890, Germany had formed the **Triple Alliance** with **Austria–Hungary** and **Italy**.

- In 1888, the new Kaiser of Germany, Wilhelm II, had great plans for German expansion. He failed to renew the agreement with **Russia**. In 1893, Russia formed the **Dual Entente** with **France**, thus ending France's isolation.

- In 1907, this Dual Entente became the **Triple Entente**, when Britain joined France and Russia because of fears over German expansion.

remember >>

In 1887, Germany's chancellor, Bismarck, had signed the Reinsurance Treaty with Russia – this promised they would not fight each other, and so deprived France of a possible ally.

practice questions

Study Source A, then describe **one** decision taken by Britain or Germany in relation to their navies in the period 1890–1914.

Fast, modern turbine engines

Guns on rotating turrets can fire shells over 9 km in any direction

Thick armour plating

Source A: The British dreadnought HMS *Barham*

Short-term causes

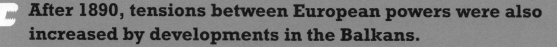

- After 1890, tensions between European powers were also increased by developments in the Balkans.

- In particular, there were serious differences between Austria–Hungary and Russia over the Balkans.

- These rising tensions were aggravated by growing nationalism, and finally led to the assassination of the Austro–Hungarian heir in Sarajevo by a Serbian nationalist group.

A   Unrest in the Balkans

>> **key fact** Problems began to arise in the Balkans from the mid-nineteenth century, when the Ottoman Empire began to decline.

- Several states wanted to take advantage of this situation, including Britain, Germany, France and Italy. The two main countries involved were **Austria–Hungary** and **Russia**.

- Austria–Hungary had a multinational empire in central Europe that bordered on the Balkans and was afraid that **growing nationalism** would lead to demands for independence. In 1878, Austria–Hungary was allowed to administer the small area of **Bosnia–Herzegovina** on behalf of Turkey.

- Russia's main concern was **access to the Mediterranean** via an ice-free port, so tended to support various nationalist Slav movements – especially the new states of **Bulgaria** and **Serbia**.

remember >>

The Balkans – covering an area that includes present-day states such as Serbia, Bulgaria and Romania – had been part of the Turkish Ottoman Empire for several centuries.

B   The Balkan Wars

>> **key fact** In 1908, the Young Turk Movement took control of the Ottoman Empire and began to modernise Turkey. This led Austria–Hungary to take over Bosnia–Herzegovina and make it part of their empire, even though Bosnia–Herzegovina wanted to join Serbia.

- **In 1911, the Young Turks fell from power** and, in the early twentieth century, growing tensions led to two wars in the Balkans.

- In 1912, the Balkan states set up the Balkan League, and the **First Balkan War** broke out. In 1912–13, a **Second Balkan War** was fought.

- **Serbia emerged from these wars as the most powerful Balkan state** – much to Austria–Hungary's alarm, who now thought that war against Serbia would soon be necessary.

C Assassination at Sarajevo

>> **key fact**  Austria–Hungary's annexation of
Bosnia–Herzegovina had angered **Russia** and caused
much disappointment and bitterness amongst **Serb
nationalists in Bosnia, who wanted to unite with Serbia.**

- One consequence of this was the creation of a Serbian terrorist
  organisation known as the **Black Hand Society**.

- By 1914, tensions in the Balkans were so great that many expected
  another war.

- The spark came on **28 June 1914**, when **Archduke Franz Ferdinand**
  – heir to the Austro-Hungarian throne – decided to visit **Sarajevo**,
  the capital of Bosnia–Herzegovina, to inspect troops.

- As he was driven through the streets in an open-top car, a series
  of attempts by Black Hand terrorists – and mistakes made by those
  responsible for his security – resulted in the **assassination** of both
  Franz Ferdinand and his wife, Sophie.

remember >>
The Black Hand
Society had links
to the Serbian
secret police.

remember >>
The terrorist
responsible
for the actual
assassinations was
Gavrilo Princip.

Practice questions

Study **Source A** below, then briefly explain why **Gavrilo Princip**
carried out the assassination of Franz Ferdinand.

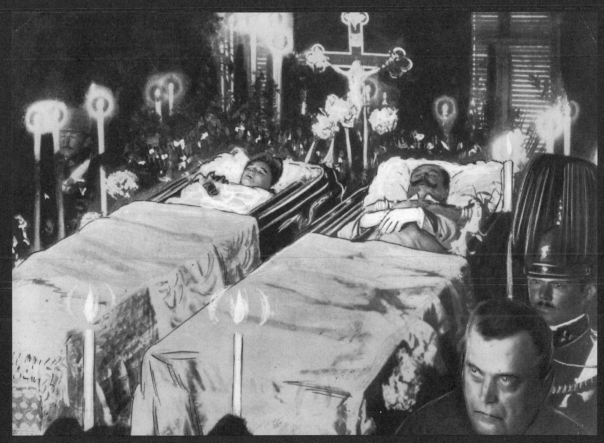

Source A: The bodies of Franz Ferdinand, Archduke of Austria, and his wife following their
assassination in Sarajevo on 28 June 1914 by Gavrilo Princip, a Serbian nationalist

The war begins

 Before 1914, nationalism and rivalry over colonies and trade led to increasing tension and an arms race between the main countries of Europe.

 This led to the formation of two opposing alliances – the Triple Entente (Allies) and the Triple Alliance (Central Powers).

 When the war began in 1914, many believed it would be 'over by Christmas', but it soon settled into the stalemate of trench warfare.

A The final steps to war

1 key fact The final steps to war were triggered when Serb nationalists assassinated Franz Ferdinand, the Archduke of Austria, in Sarajevo, Bosnia, in June 1914.

Nationalism in the Balkans had been a problem for some time, and had been made worse by the rival ambitions of **Austria**, **Russia** and **Germany**, all of whom wished to expand in the area.	In July, the Kaiser let Austria know it would have German backing in any war with Serbia. When **Austria declared war on Serbia on 28 July, Russia began to mobilise and refused a German demand to stop.**	By 3 August 1914, Germany and Austria had declared war on Russia and France. Italy, part of the Triple Alliance, stayed neutral in 1914 and later joined the Triple Entente in 1915.

2 key fact On 4 August 1914, Britain declared war on Germany after German forces (following their Schlieffen Plan) had invaded Belgium.

The Schlieffen Plan had been designed to enable Germany to survive a **two-front war**, by invading France through Belgium before Russia could mobilise.

3 key fact The Schlieffen Plan failed for three reasons.

(i) **The Russian army mobilised more quickly than expected**, so German troops had to be sent from the attack on France to go to the Eastern Front.

(ii) **Belgium put up unexpected resistance** – this slowed the German advance into France.

(iii) **The British Expeditionary Force (BEF) joined French forces** in a successful counter-attack on the River Marne. This stopped the Germans from capturing Paris, and forced them to retreat.

B The power blocs

This is how the great powers lined up during the First World War:

Triple Entente (Allies)	Triple Alliance (Central Powers)
Britain	Germany
France	Austria
Russia (until 1917)	Turkey
Italy (after 1915)	Italy (until 1915)
USA (after 1917)	
Japan	

C Stalemate

>> key fact Both sides then began a 'race to the sea', in order to be the first to capture the Channel ports. By November 1914, a line of trenches on the Western Front stretched over 470 kilometres, from the North Sea to Switzerland.

- Both armies were approximately equal in size, and their **weapons** (machine guns, heavy artillery) **were more defensive than offensive**. Soon, a **stalemate** existed on the Western Front as the war became a series of attacks on the enemy trenches.

- There were several major battles, including Ypres (1915), Verdun and the Somme (1916) and Passchendaele (1917). However, despite heavy casualties, these battles failed to bring about a breakthrough, or even to gain much ground.

- New tactics and weapons (artillery barrages, gas, tanks, planes) failed to break the stalemate as each side quickly copied the other side's tactics.

- So the First World War quickly became a **war of attrition**, in which each side tried to destroy more of the enemy than it lost itself.

>> practice questions

1 Why did Britain declare war on Germany?

2 How did the weapons used in the First World War help to create a stalemate?

Warfare

- Attacks were preceded by heavy artillery barrages that sometimes lasted for days.

- Before an attack, whistles were blown; then the troops advanced across no-man's land to attack the enemy trenches – this was known as 'going over the top'.

- Both sides used new tactics (e.g. prolonged heavy artillery barrages) to try to break the stalemate on the Western Front. However, when these failed, new technology was also put to the test.

A   The trenches

① key fact   There were four main types of trenches.

- Behind the **frontline** trenches (from which attacks were made) were **support** trenches and, behind them, **reserve** trenches.

- These three types of trenches were connected by **communications** trenches.

- German trenches tended to be better constructed and so gave better protection from artillery barrages.

> **remember >>**
> No-man's land was the ground that separated opposing trenches.

② key fact   Conditions in the trenches soon became dreadful as the heavy shelling destroyed drainage systems.

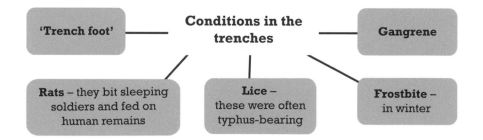

'Trench foot' — Conditions in the trenches — Gangrene

Rats – they bit sleeping soldiers and fed on human remains

Lice – these were often typhus-bearing

Frostbite – in winter

Shelling and rain soon turned the trenches and no-man's land into a sea of mud. Many wounded soldiers drowned in the numerous shell craters.

③ key fact   The prolonged shelling, gas attacks and awful conditions led soldiers to suffer nervous breakdowns.

At first, soldiers who had breakdowns were often shot for desertion or refusal to obey orders under fire. Later, this psychological disturbance was recognised as **shell-shock**, and affected soldiers received medical treatment.

8

B Weapons

1 **key fact** On land, some weapons (such as machine guns) actually led to a more defensive war. However, there were many important new developments in weaponry for use on land, at sea and in the air.

remember >>
You need to be able to explain why these new weapons failed to break the stalemate on the Western Front.

Land	Sea	Air
Gas – the first use of poison gas (chlorine) was by the Germans in 1915. Phosgene and mustard gas were also used later by both sides. Despite some early successes, **the use of gas was dependent on the weather**, so army commanders remained doubtful about its effectiveness. Gas masks were developed to counter the effects of gas.	**Dreadnoughts** – new, larger and more powerful battleships, developed by both sides before 1914. However, they only fought one major battle (Jutland, 1916).	**Planes** – at first, planes were used for observation (scouting). Later, they attacked enemy trenches with machine guns and bombs. Aerial fights ('dog fights') took place.
Tanks – these were developed by the British navy in 1915, as the army was not interested. They were first used in 1916 at the Battle of the Somme. **Early problems (mud, heat and breakdowns) meant generals were not very interested in their use.** Although used more seriously in the Battle of Cambrai in 1917, they were not fully used until 1918.	**Submarines** – the German U-boats destroyed much British shipping (25 per cent by April 1917) and were a serious threat.	**Airships** – German Zeppelins bombed British towns and cities, but they had poor navigation and were difficult to use in bad weather.

2 **key fact** However, many of these developments failed to produce the decisive breakthrough.

- Both sides made similar advances or copied their enemy's inventions. Also, the two sides developed ways of combating the new technology.

- Britain countered German U-boats with:

  - **hydrophones** – these detected submarines so that depth charges could then destroy the U-boats

  - **a convoy system** – merchant ships sailed together in zigzag patterns and were protected by destroyers and torpedo boats. This was more effective than hydrophones – **by November 1918, British merchant losses had dropped to 4 per cent**.

- Britain dealt with Zeppelins by improving air defences, so, from 1916, Germany was forced to switch to night-bombers.

>> practice questions

1 Describe the impact the German U-boat campaign had on Britain.

2 Explain how Britain dealt with the problems caused by U-boats.

The end of the war

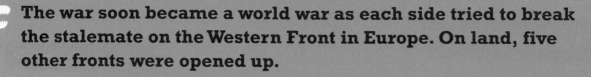

- ● The war soon became a world war as each side tried to break the stalemate on the Western Front in Europe. On land, five other fronts were opened up.

- ● There was also fighting at sea and in the air.

- ● In 1917, important changes to the membership of the Triple Entente took place, with the USA joining and Russia pulling out.

A Other land fronts

Eastern Front	Middle East	East Africa
• **Austria–Hungary** heavily defeated the Russians at Tannenberg and Mausarian Lakes in 1914. However, there was no trench warfare. Russia's **Brusilov Offensive** in June 1916 soon collapsed; by the end of 1916, German troops occupied large areas of Russia. • In the **Balkans**, there was heavy fighting during the Gallipoli campaign when the **Allies tried to capture the Dardanelles and so weaken Germany's ally, Turkey**. • In December 1915, the Allies were forced to withdraw. There was also fighting against Bulgaria in the Salonika campaign. • The **Italian Front** saw bitter fighting between Italy **(which switched to the Allies in 1915)** and Austria–Hungary and Germany. Italian losses were heavy at the Battle of Caporetto, 1917.	• The Allies tried to protect oil supplies threatened by Turkey. • The main fighting was in Mesopotamia (Iraq) and in Palestine, where the Arabs revolted against Turkish rule.	• The Allies quickly took Germany's colonies, although the war here continued until 1918.

>> **key fact** Both Britain and Germany depended on importing food and materials. Therefore, using powerful navies to protect sea routes and merchant ships was vital.

- • At first, German U-boats were a serious problem, but **Britain soon imposed a naval blockade of all German ports**.

- • In the air, aeroplanes were used against enemy trenches. 'Dog fights' between opposing airforces also took place.

remember >>

You need to be able to identify the aims of the Allied campaigns in Gallipoli and in the Middle East.

B   The stalemate is broken

1 **key fact** From March 1917, revolution in Russia weakened the war effort of Britain and France's ally.

- However, in April 1917, the USA joined the Allies. Allied morale was boosted.

- Russia's involvement in the war was finally ended by the Treaty of Brest-Litovsk with Germany in March 1918. **This allowed Germany to switch most of its troops from the Eastern to the Western Front.**

- Hindenburg and Ludendorff, the German commanders, decided to use these extra troops before US forces could be built up.

2 **key fact** The German Spring (Ludendorff) Offensive, using specially trained and more mobile Stormtroopers, was successful at first, and seemed to have ended the stalemate.

- But the Allies regrouped and, with extra US troops, counter-attacked in August. **This (with the first really effective use of tanks) began to push the Germans back.**

- Several factors caused this. The Germans had no overall plan, no reserves and only limited supplies. They advanced so quickly that they tired themselves out. The Allies, however, were well supplied and reinforced with fresh US troops.

- With Britain's naval blockade, and mutiny and revolution threatening in Germany, Hindenburg and Ludendorff decided Germany would have to surrender. **The armistice took effect on 11 November 1918.**

remember >>

During 1915 and 1916, despite new weapons, the stalemate on the Western Front continued.

>> practice questions

Study Sources A and B below, then answer the questions that follow.

Source A: Civilian deaths in Germany, 1915–18

Source B: Civilians in Berlin scavenging for food, 1918

1 How far does Source B support the evidence of Source A?

2 How useful is Source B as historical evidence of the impact of the Allied naval blockade on German civilians during the war? Explain your answer.

exam tip >>

Don't forget to make clear references to all the sources mentioned.

The difficulties of peace-making

- The defeated members of the Central Powers were excluded from the peace conferences, which began in January 1919.

- The USA, Britain and France (the Big Three) made most of the decisions about the peace treaties.

- However, the Big Three had different aims – this caused problems when they began to draw up the treaties. Another problem was that the war had ended before serious discussions had taken place.

A Differing aims of the Big Three

USA	Britain	France
President Woodrow Wilson had issued his Fourteen Points in January 1918 as the basis of a peace treaty to end the war.	Many people in Britain wanted Germany to be punished, and Lloyd George wanted to enlarge the British empire by taking Germany's colonies. Lloyd George had been re-elected in 1918 after an election in which slogans such as 'Hang the Kaiser!' and 'Make Germany pay!' had been common.	Clemenceau (nicknamed 'The Tiger'), wanted to make Germany weak.
He wanted **self-determination** for all nationalities and the establishment of a **League of Nations** to prevent future wars.		He wanted to do this by imposing **huge compensation** for damage and war debts, taking large parts of German territory and industry, and forcing almost total disarmament on defeated Germany.
Overall, President Wilson wanted a just peace.	**Overall, Lloyd George wanted a compromise peace** (to avoid Germany seeking revenge, so that Germany could resume trade with Britain, and to keep Germany strong enough to resist Communism).	**Overall, Clemenceau wanted a harsh peace**, as France had suffered great destruction during the war. At first, though, he had hoped the USA would cancel France's war debts. But Wilson refused, so Clemenceau decided to take money from Germany instead.

>> **key fact** The biggest problem was Germany – the Allies wanted to be sure Germany would not be strong enough to fight another war.

There was also **political chaos in Germany** as workers' risings and mutinies in the armed forces (some inspired by the Bolshevik Revolution in Russia) had led the Kaiser to flee, and left the new government weak.

remember >>

Lloyd George and Clemenceau thought Wilson was too idealistic. Because Wilson was ill during the conferences, and was also losing control of the US Congress, he was forced to make many concessions.

B Other problems

There were also several other problems that made peace-making difficult.

- In Central and Eastern Europe, **nationalism was breaking up the Austro-Hungarian empire** and leading to the formation of independent but weak countries (Poland, Czechoslovakia and Yugoslavia). In Hungary, a Communist revolution broke out.

- Large areas of Europe were suffering from **near-starvation and economic collapse** (especially Germany, as the Allied blockade remained in force). Millions of people died from a flu epidemic.

- Other countries, such as Italy and Japan (as well as groups such as the Jews and Arabs), had been promised land in secret deals and now wanted their rewards. But some of these were **conflicting promises, or were opposed by Wilson**.

Study Sources A and B below, then answer the questions that follow.

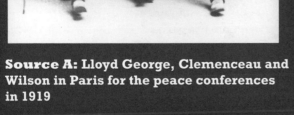

Source A: Lloyd George, Clemenceau and Wilson in Paris for the peace conferences in 1919

> England and France have not the same views with respect to peace that we have by any means. When the war is over we can force them to our way of thinking because by that time they will, among other things, be financially in our hands.

Source B: The views of US President Woodrow Wilson in 1917, written in a private note

1 **Name the three countries represented by the men in Source A.**

2 **In Source B, why did Wilson think England and France would be 'financially in the hands' of the USA by the time the First World War was over?**

3 **How far do you trust Source B as evidence of the views of the US government?**

remember >>

Many people, especially in France and Belgium, wanted revenge on Germany for the human and economic costs of the war. Millions had been killed or horribly wounded, and many farms, factories, roads and railways had been destroyed.

The Treaty of Versailles

- Five separate peace treaties were signed between the Allies and the members of the defeated Central Powers. The most important was the Treaty of Versailles with Germany, signed in June 1919.

- Germany was not involved in the discussions, and was only given days to agree – if Germany refused, the war would resume.

- So most Germans saw the treaty as a diktat (dictated peace).

A   The details

1 key fact Germany lost 10 per cent of its lands in Europe, along with 12.5 per cent of its population, 16 per cent of its coalfields and 50 per cent of its iron and steel industries.

remember >>

Germany was also forced to sign a 'War Guilt Clause' accepting total responsibility for starting the war and agreeing to pay reparations – set at £6.6 billion in 1921.

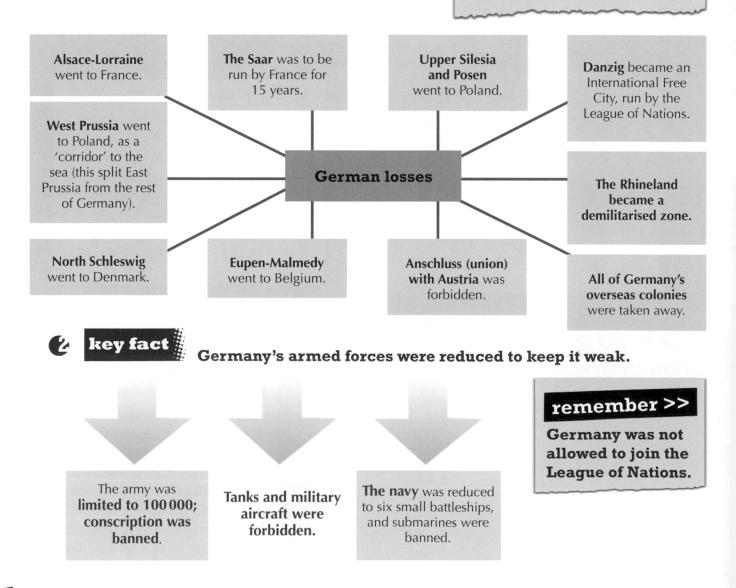

Alsace-Lorraine went to France.

The Saar was to be run by France for 15 years.

Upper Silesia and Posen went to Poland.

Danzig became an International Free City, run by the League of Nations.

West Prussia went to Poland, as a 'corridor' to the sea (this split East Prussia from the rest of Germany).

German losses

The Rhineland became a demilitarised zone.

North Schleswig went to Denmark.

Eupen-Malmedy went to Belgium.

Anschluss (union) with Austria was forbidden.

All of Germany's overseas colonies were taken away.

2 key fact Germany's armed forces were reduced to keep it weak.

remember >>

Germany was not allowed to join the League of Nations.

The army was limited to 100 000; conscription was banned.

Tanks and military aircraft were forbidden.

The navy was reduced to six small battleships, and submarines were banned.

B   The German reaction

>> **key fact** Because Germany was not given an opportunity to influence the terms, it objected to the way in which the Treaty of Versailles was forced on the nation.

Most Germans resented:

- the loss of land, industry, population and all their colonies

- the lack of self-determination for Germans and German-speakers in the new countries formed from the Austro-Hungarian empire

- the military restrictions imposed on their armed forces, and their exclusion from the League of Nations

- the 'War Guilt Clause', and the amount of reparations.

C   How unfair was the treaty?

Historians are divided over how unfair the treaty was.

- **Unfair**: it was not based on Wilson's Fourteen Points; it punished the German people, who had had little influence over the Kaiser and the military commanders.

remember >>

The new German government had thought the treaty would be based on Wilson's Fourteen Points.

- **Fair**: Germany did not lose that much territory (far less than it took from Russia in the Treaty of Brest-Litovsk in 1918); the German economy revived quickly in the second half of the 1920s; reparations were reduced progressively after 1919; throughout the 1920s, Germany managed to avoid complying with many of the military restrictions imposed by the Treaty of Versailles.

>> practice questions

Study Sources A and B below, then answer the question that follows.

PEACE AND FUTURE CANNON FODDER

The Tiger : "Curious ! I seem to hear a child weeping !"

Source A:
A British cartoon about the Treaty of Versailles produced in 1919

Source B:
A British journalist's view of the Treaty of Versailles, 1929

It was a peace of vengeance.

It reeked with injustice. It was incapable of fulfilment. It sowed a thousand seeds from which new wars might spring …

The absurdity, the wild impossibility, of extracting that vast tribute (reparations) from the defeated enemy … ought to have been obvious to the most ignorant schoolboy.

What can you learn from these two sources about the Treaty of Versailles?

Use the sources and your own knowledge to explain your answer.

Assessing the treaties

- Germany's defeated allies (Austria, Hungary, Bulgaria and Turkey) were dealt with by four separate treaties.

- In general, the treaties contributed to the disruption of the economies of Central and Eastern Europe, and so led to reduced trade after the war.

- The Successor States contained many different national groups, some of which did not want to be part of them. These states were also weak in military terms.

A The other treaties

① key fact The Austro-Hungarian empire was split into several separate countries (known as the Successor States), with Austria and Hungary becoming two separate countries. Large areas of the Habsburg empire, containing over three million German-speakers, were given to Czechoslovakia and Poland.

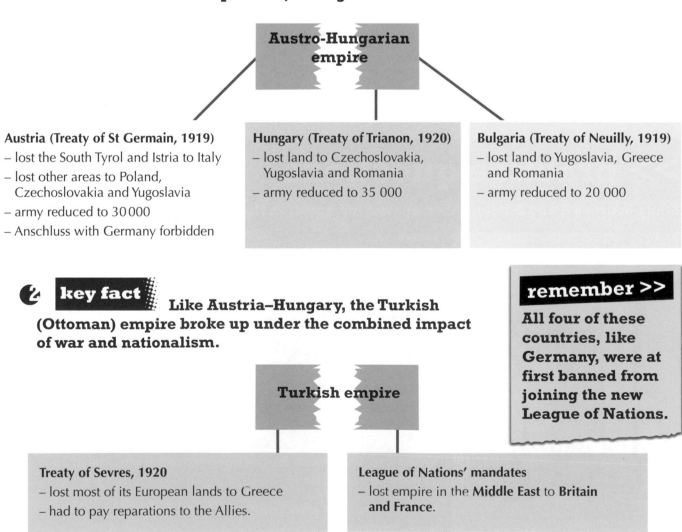

Austro-Hungarian empire

Austria (Treaty of St Germain, 1919)
- lost the South Tyrol and Istria to Italy
- lost other areas to Poland, Czechoslovakia and Yugoslavia
- army reduced to 30 000
- Anschluss with Germany forbidden

Hungary (Treaty of Trianon, 1920)
- lost land to Czechoslovakia, Yugoslavia and Romania
- army reduced to 35 000

Bulgaria (Treaty of Neuilly, 1919)
- lost land to Yugoslavia, Greece and Romania
- army reduced to 20 000

② key fact Like Austria–Hungary, the Turkish (Ottoman) empire broke up under the combined impact of war and nationalism.

> **remember >>**
>
> All four of these countries, like Germany, were at first banned from joining the new League of Nations.

Turkish empire

Treaty of Sevres, 1920
- lost most of its European lands to Greece
- had to pay reparations to the Allies.

League of Nations' mandates
- lost empire in the **Middle East** to **Britain and France**.

B How successful were the peace treaties?

①  **key fact** **Many of the defeated countries of the Central Powers were unhappy with the treaties.**

- Because of the short-lived Communist uprising, a treaty wasn't signed with **Hungary** until 1920, following the brutal suppression of the uprising. The new right-wing dictatorship resented the loss of territory (about 60 per cent) and about 11 million of its citizens.

- In **Turkey**, the harsh Treaty of Sevres led to a nationalist revolt (led by Mustafa Kemal) that overthrew the sultan. Kemal then attacked Greece to regain lost land. The Allies agreed to return most of this land in the **Treaty of Lausanne, 1923**.

② **key fact** **Some of the Allies were also unhappy with the treaties.**

- **Italy** was angry that much of the land it had been promised by the secret Treaty of London, 1915, went to Yugoslavia.

- **France** felt Germany had not been weakened enough. France needed reparations to pay off its war debts to the USA (which the USA refused to cancel).

- **Britain**, however, soon thought that the Treaty of Versailles had been too tough on Germany and did not support France's hard-line approach.

Practice questions

Study Source A, then answer the question that follows.

Does this source provide enough evidence to assess the attitudes of French governments towards Germany after the First World War? Use the source and your own knowledge to explain your answer.

Source A:
A French poster produced after the First World War. (The text says: 'Murderers always return to the scenes of their crime.')

exam tip >>

Make sure you give precise references to the information/views presented by the source. Don't forget to use your own knowledge to show why this source does not provide enough evidence – and make sure you give precise (NOT vague) facts.

remember >>

Britain and France had different ideas on how Germany should be treated. This would lead to difficulties in the period 1919–39.

Establishment of the League

- The last of Wilson's Fourteen Points concerned the setting up of a League of Nations.

- The first 26 sections of all the peace treaties dealt with the League's establishment. Its rules were known as the Covenant.

- Despite the hopes surrounding the establishment of the League of Nations, there were many weaknesses. During the 1920s, and especially the 1930s, these weaknesses began to undermine its effectiveness.

A Organisation

① key fact
The League's headquarters were in Geneva, in neutral Switzerland.

- Membership was open to all countries except **the defeated Central Powers, who were not allowed to join** until they had proved their commitment to peaceful solutions.

- **Communist Russia** was also not allowed to join.

remember >>

The League's commissions also tried to control the arms trade, illegal drugs and the freedom of trade and communications.

LEAGUE OF NATIONS

Aims

To **prevent war** by solving problems by negotiation, and by guaranteeing each country's borders – by force, if necessary (known as **collective security**)

To bring about **disarmament**

Organisation

The Assembly met once a year, and all member states had one vote.

The Court of International Justice

The Council was made up of the **Big Four** (Britain, France, Italy and Japan) as permanent members, plus four smaller countries elected at intervals by the Assembly.

The Secretariat carried out the routine administration of the League's work.

Methods

Pressure of **world opinion**

Economic sanctions (trade bans) by all member countries

Force as a last resort

② key fact
The League's aims included a commitment to improve health, education and living and working conditions.

This was because poverty and injustice were felt to be important factors in causing wars. Special commissions included the Commission for Refugees and the ILO.

B Weaknesses

 key fact One of the League's biggest problems concerned its membership.

- Three of the most important countries were not members. These were the **USA**, **Russia** and **Germany**.

- Although Wilson (a Democrat) had pushed hard for the League to be set up, the idea was not popular in the USA. He lost control of Congress to the Republicans in 1918, and they refused to ratify US membership.

- Russia did not belong to the League (because it had a Communist government).

- Germany was prevented from joining as part of its punishment after the war.

key fact The League was dominated by Britain and France.

As a result, the defeated and excluded countries had little respect for its decisions. Instead, they saw it as a **victors' club** or (in the case of Russia) a **capitalists' club**.

key fact The League was further weakened by the fact that Britain and France did not agree on what should happen in Europe, and so did not always cooperate.

- Britain was more **interested in its empire** and did not want France to dominate Europe.

- France, on the other hand, wanted to **prevent Germany becoming economically and militarily strong again**. French fears were strengthened by Britain's refusal to give firm guarantees of military assistance in the event of war.

- Because Britain did not want to act as the **policeman of the world**, it refused to agree to the League having its own army.

>> practice questions

Study Source A, then answer the questions that follow.

1 How far does this source explain why the non-membership of the USA was a weakness for the League of Nations?

2 Which other important countries were at first denied membership of the League?

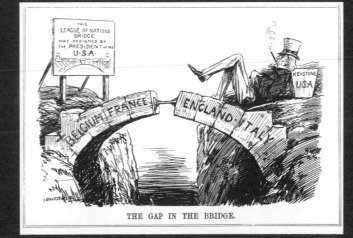

Source A: Cartoon showing the formation and membership of the League of Nations, published in a British magazine

The League in the 1920s

- The League was able to settle several disputes in the 1920s, although these tended not to involve powerful countries.

- However, the League also had several failures in the 1920s – these usually had to do with disputes involving strong countries.

A   Successes

1920 – **Yugoslavia's invasion of Albania**

1921 – **Upper Silesia,** between Poland and Germany, and the **Aaland Islands,** between Finland and Sweden

1925 – **Greece's invasion of Bulgaria**

Resolving disputes

LEAGUE OF NATIONS

successes

remember >>

The League also did much good work through its special commissions. In particular, many refugees from the war were helped to return home; its Health Committee did much to reduce disease across the world; it helped stop slave labour and the use of dangerous chemicals in some places.

Important agreements

Peace and disarmament

One important achievement of the League came in 1926, when **Germany was allowed to join.**

While most agreements were the result of direct diplomacy or the work of the **Conference of Ambassadors** (the Big Four), the League did much to create the atmosphere in which such agreements could be made.

Locarno Pact, 1925 – Germany accepted its western borders as set out in the Treaty of Versailles, and agreed that any changes to its eastern borders should be by discussion.

Kellogg–Briand Pact, 1928 – forty-five countries agreed never to resort to war as a way of resolving disputes

B Failures

remember >>

As a result of these failures, some people were already criticising the League's inability to prevent or end aggression before the end of the 1920s.

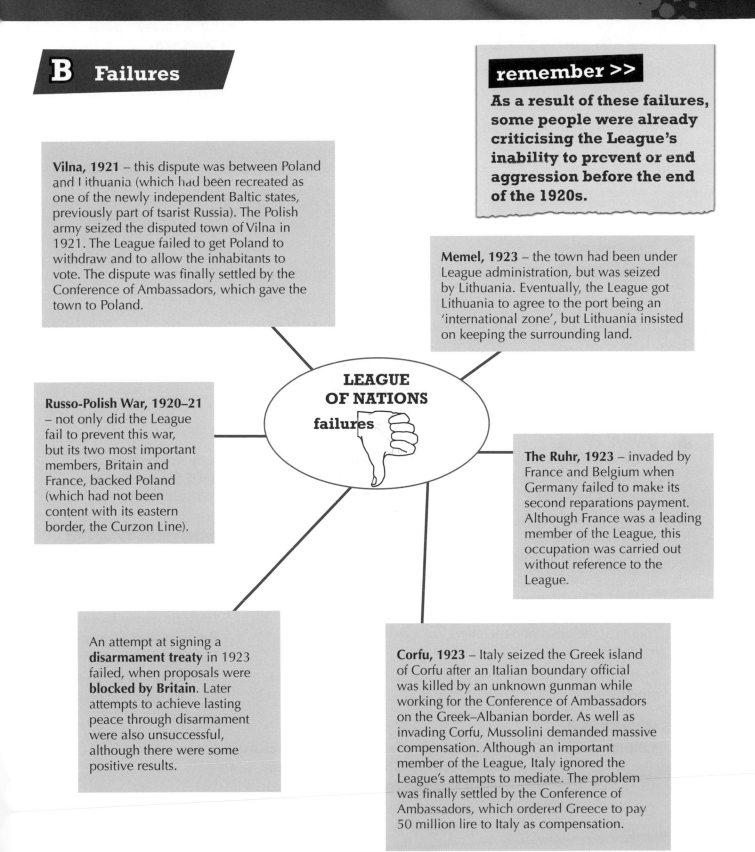

Vilna, 1921 – this dispute was between Poland and Lithuania (which had been recreated as one of the newly independent Baltic states, previously part of tsarist Russia). The Polish army seized the disputed town of Vilna in 1921. The League failed to get Poland to withdraw and to allow the inhabitants to vote. The dispute was finally settled by the Conference of Ambassadors, which gave the town to Poland.

Memel, 1923 – the town had been under League administration, but was seized by Lithuania. Eventually, the League got Lithuania to agree to the port being an 'international zone', but Lithuania insisted on keeping the surrounding land.

Russo-Polish War, 1920–21 – not only did the League fail to prevent this war, but its two most important members, Britain and France, backed Poland (which had not been content with its eastern border, the Curzon Line).

LEAGUE OF NATIONS failures

The Ruhr, 1923 – invaded by France and Belgium when Germany failed to make its second reparations payment. Although France was a leading member of the League, this occupation was carried out without reference to the League.

An attempt at signing a **disarmament treaty** in 1923 failed, when proposals were **blocked by Britain**. Later attempts to achieve lasting peace through disarmament were also unsuccessful, although there were some positive results.

Corfu, 1923 – Italy seized the Greek island of Corfu after an Italian boundary official was killed by an unknown gunman while working for the Conference of Ambassadors on the Greek–Albanian border. As well as invading Corfu, Mussolini demanded massive compensation. Although an important member of the League, Italy ignored the League's attempts to mediate. The problem was finally settled by the Conference of Ambassadors, which ordered Greece to pay 50 million lire to Italy as compensation.

>> practice questions

1   What important failure, involving Italy, did the League have in 1923?

2   How was this dispute resolved eventually?

The League in the 1930s

◀ Despite some successes in the 1920s, the League had not established itself as the main body for settling disputes, and its most important members often followed different policies.

◀ By 1936, the League had suffered three serious failures.

A Successes

>> **key fact** The League did have some success in the 1930s.

- A border dispute between **Colombia and Peru** was settled by the League in 1932.

- The **Soviet Union** became a member of the League in 1934.

B Failures

1 key fact However, the weaknesses of the League were made worse by the impact of the Great Depression, which followed the Wall Street Crash in the USA in 1929.

- As a result, many countries, such as **Italy, Japan and Germany**, came to be ruled by extreme nationalist governments that adopted **aggressive foreign policies** to solve their economic problems.

- Also, many other countries put their economic interests first, and so were **reluctant to impose economic sanctions** on an aggressive country in case it harmed their own trade. These countries included **non-members**, such as the USA, as well as **members**, such as Britain and France.

- By the mid-1930s, many people felt the League was unable to prevent aggression.

remember >>

The weaknesses of the League were the lack of unity between Britain and France, the absence of the USA and the lack of its own armed forces.

2 key fact The League's first serious failure came in September 1931, when Japan invaded Manchuria, a Chinese province. Both Japan and China were League members.

The League ordered Japan to withdraw and the Japanese government agreed, but their army refused.	In December 1931, the League set up the **Lytton Commission** to investigate but, by February 1932, all of Manchuria had been occupied and it was renamed 'Manchukuo'.	The Lytton Report, November 1932, ordered Japan to withdraw. The report was accepted by the League but **Japan simply left the League in February 1933.**

③ **key fact** The next important failure was the World Disarmament Conference, which lasted from 1932–3.

This conference was a continuation of the failed attempt in 1923.

However, **Hitler** demanded '**equality of treatment**' for Germany – either all countries should disarm to the level imposed on Germany in 1919, or Germany should be allowed to match the levels of other countries.

Agreement could not be reached, and **Hitler took Germany out of the Conference and the League**.

④ **key fact** Another serious set-back for the League came in October 1935, when Fascist Italy invaded Abyssinia.

Britain and France saw Italy as an ally against Germany, so they took no real action. The Suez Canal was not closed to Italian supply ships, and oil, coal and steel were not in the trade sanctions imposed by the League.

Non-members, such as the USA and Nazi Germany, continued to trade with Italy.

Britain and France drew up the secret **Hoare–Laval Pact** to give two-thirds of Abyssinia to Italy.

Although the League ended all sanctions in July 1936, **Italy left the League in December 1937**.

It was too late – in May 1936, Italy renamed Abyssinia 'Ethiopia'.

This collapsed and, in December 1936, the League finally placed sanctions on oil and petrol.

>> practice questions

Study Source A below, then answer the question that follows.

Source A: British cartoon about the League of Nation's policy on the Japanese invasion of Manchuria, 1931

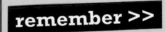
remember >>

Even biased or unreliable sources can be useful.

How useful is Source A as historical evidence of how the League of Nations dealt with the crisis in Manchuria? Explain your answer.

The end of tsarist Russia

- Russia was ruled by a tsar (emperor) who had absolute power. There was no democracy.

- Most of the land was owned by a few noble families, and over 80 per cent of the population were poor, illiterate peasants.

- In 1914, Nicholas II decided to get involved in the First World War.

- In March 1917, a revolution broke out, which resulted in the abdication of the Tsar.

A   Russia before 1914

1 key fact
Some industrialisation had begun in the 1890s, but only as a result of foreign investment. This 'Great Spurt' had been due mainly to Sergei Witte, Minister of Finance from 1893–1903 and Prime Minister from 1903–06.

- Russian factories were large and working conditions were poor – many of the workers were recent illiterate migrants from rural Russia.

- After 1900, an industrial depression and bad harvests led to wage cuts, unemployment and high food prices.

- In 1904, the Tsar, Nicholas II, declared war on Japan. But the **Russo-Japanese War** went badly for Russia.

2 key fact
A peaceful demonstration in January 1905 was fired on by soldiers and this 'Bloody Sunday' sparked off the 1905 Revolution.

- At first, those who wanted change united against the Tsar.

- On the advice of Witte, the Tsar issued the **October Manifesto**, which promised a **Duma** (parliament) and free speech – Witte believed this would split those opposing the Tsar.

- The **Kadets** ended their opposition, and the Tsar then used the army to crush the workers and their **soviet** (strike committee), which had been set up in **St Petersburg**.

remember >>

The Kadets, or Constitutional Democrats, were middle-class liberals.

3 key fact
The Tsar went back on his promises, giving little power to the Duma and greater representation to the rich.

- When the Duma criticised the Tsar's actions, he dismissed it and ordered new elections. By 1912, he was back to ruling without a Duma.

- After 1906, the Tsar's new chief minister, **Peter Stolypin**, carried out a harsh repression, in which many were hanged. However, as well as reducing opposition, he also began land reform to win the support of better-off peasants.

B The impact of the First World War

1 key fact
In 1911, Stolypin was assassinated. Between 1911–14, protests and strikes began to increase. Nicholas II then took Russia into the First World War.

remember >>

Those who opposed the Tsar included the Social Democrats – a Marxist party that, in 1903, had split into Menshevik and Bolshevik factions, and that was most popular with factory workers.

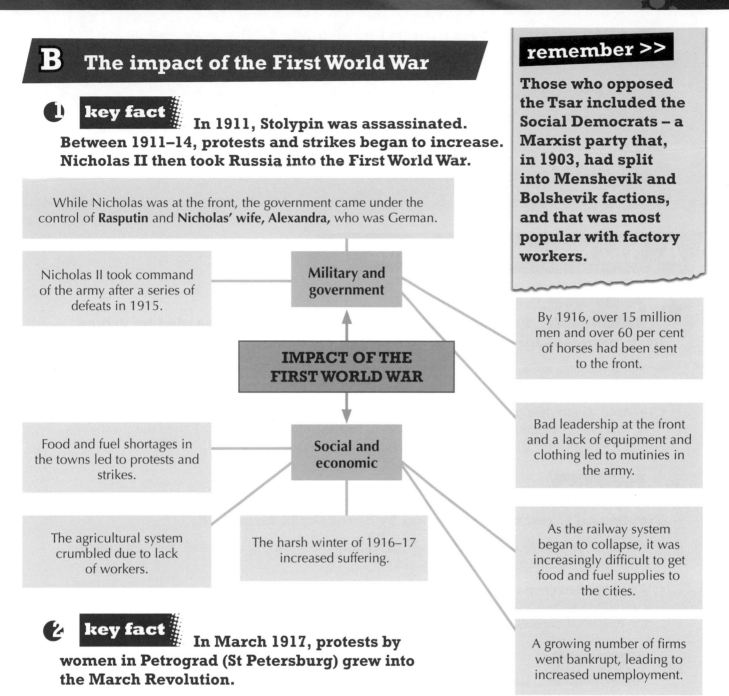

While Nicholas was at the front, the government came under the control of **Rasputin** and **Nicholas' wife, Alexandra,** who was German.

Nicholas II took command of the army after a series of defeats in 1915.

Military and government

IMPACT OF THE FIRST WORLD WAR

By 1916, over 15 million men and over 60 per cent of horses had been sent to the front.

Food and fuel shortages in the towns led to protests and strikes.

Social and economic

Bad leadership at the front and a lack of equipment and clothing led to mutinies in the army.

The agricultural system crumbled due to lack of workers.

The harsh winter of 1916–17 increased suffering.

As the railway system began to collapse, it was increasingly difficult to get food and fuel supplies to the cities.

A growing number of firms went bankrupt, leading to increased unemployment.

2 key fact
In March 1917, protests by women in Petrograd (St Petersburg) grew into the March Revolution.

- The police lost control, and many soldiers joined the demonstrators – on 15 March, **Nicholas abdicated**.

- A **Provisional Government** (temporary, but unelected) was set up by some members of the Duma. At the same time, workers and soldiers elected the Petrograd Soviet (reviving the one formed in 1905). This was at first dominated by the Socialist Revolutionary Party (SRs) and the Mensheviks, who supported the Provisional Government.

- From March to November 1917, **dual power** existed between the Russian Provisional Government and the Petrograd Soviet – but the Soviet's **Order No. 1** said that the government's orders were only to be obeyed if they agreed with Soviet decisions.

>> practice questions

1 Why did the Tsar decide to involve Russia in the First World War?

2 What do you understand by the term 'dual power'?

The Bolsheviks win power

- The Provisional Government kept Russia in the war and postponed important reforms until after the war.

- This was very unpopular and, in November, a second revolution overthrow the Provisional Government.

- Soon a civil war had broken out between Reds (Communists) and Whites (anti-Communists).

A The November Revolution

1 key fact The unelected Provisional Government, headed by Prince Lvov, promised free elections for a proper parliament, but no date was set.

- Many workers, soldiers and peasants were angry that Russia continued in the First World War, and at the lack of land reform.

- In April, **Lenin** (leader of the Bolsheviks) returned from exile. His **April Theses** encouraged workers and peasants to take action. In May, **Trotsky** returned. He now joined the Bolsheviks, and soon became an important Bolshevik spokesperson.

2 key fact In July, soldiers and workers tried to overthrow the Provisional Government, now led by Kerensky (a former SR).

- Although the Bolsheviks had not planned the **July Days**, Kerensky banned them and arrested their leaders – Lenin escaped to Finland.

- An **attempted coup** in September 1917 by **General Lavr Kornilov** (C-in-C) led Kerensky to panic. He released the Bolsheviks, and gave weapons to their Red Guards. The coup collapsed, and the Bolsheviks' popularity increased.

3 key fact Lenin decided on a second revolution to overthrow Kerensky.

- Some Bolsheviks were opposed, but their Central Committee finally voted in favour.

- Most of the organisation for the revolution was done by Trotsky, recently elected as chair of the Soviet's **Military Revolutionary Committee (MRC)**.

- On 6–7 November 1917, Bolshevik Red Guards and MRC soldiers overthrew Kerensky in the **November Revolution**. Power then passed to the **All-Russian Congress of Soviets**, which had just opened and had a Bolshevik majority. It elected a government (**Sovnarkom**), with Lenin as Chairman (Prime Minister).

- Land was taken from the nobility, but the Peasants' Congress rejected the Bolshevik idea of nationalising the land. The All-Russian Congress voted for an end to the war.

- In December, the SRs split into Left and Right, with the **Left SR Party joining the Bolsheviks in a coalition government**. The elections to the Constituent Assembly took place before the SR split, with most peasants supporting the Left SR policies on land and war.

> **remember >>**
>
> Lenin's 'April Theses' contained two slogans – 'Peace, Bread and Land' and 'All power to the soviets'.

B The Civil War

① key fact The Constituent Assembly met in January 1918 but was immediately closed down, because the Kadets and other groups opposed to the November Revolution threatened counter-revolution.

- The **Cheka** was set up to deal with threats of counter-revolution.

- The biggest problem was **ending the war**. Many peasant soldiers were deserting to share out the nobles' lands, and large parts of Russia were occupied by German troops.

- Lenin wanted an immediate peace, but others in the government disagreed. The **Treaty of Brest-Litovsk**, signed in **March 1918**, forced Russia to give up much land and resources.

- The Left SRs left the coalition in protest. By then, a **civil war** had broken out between **Reds** (Communists) and **Whites** (anti-Communists). Several Allied armies intervened on the side of the Whites. Both sides resorted to terror at times.

- The Reds seemed likely to lose, because the Whites had several well-equipped armies and controlled most of Russia. The Communists just had the Red Guards and controlled only the **central parts** of Russia.

② key fact Trotsky, as Commissar of War, used conscription and many ex-tsarist officers to quickly build up a large and efficient Red Army.

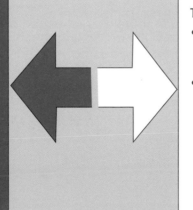

The Reds
- United.
- Good control of the centre (including main railways and factories), which allowed them to move troops and supplies quickly from one front to another.

The Whites
- Leaders often refused to cooperate with each other.
- By 1920, the Whites were on the verge of total defeat, but then Poland invaded. This war was ended by the Treaty of Riga in 1921.

>> practice questions

1 **Which Bolshevik leader was in charge of the Red Army?**

2 **Give three reasons why the Reds won the Civil War.**

Economic policies under Lenin

- At first, the Communists thought factories would still have to be run by their private owners (state capitalism).

- But when the Civil War began, the Communists introduced emergency economic measures known as War Communism.

- This was replaced in 1921 by the New Economic Policy – this was controversial as it involved a partial return to capitalism.

A War Communism

>> **key fact** The Communists wanted state-owned farms and state capitalism in the factories. But the peasants took over the land for themselves, while workers occupied factories and placed them under workers' control, so the government introduced War Communism.

remember >>

During the Civil War, the Communists had begun to restrict soviet democracy by limiting elections and banning some political groups, especially those that were known to have assassinated Communist officials.

WAR COMMUNISM

- To prevent the near collapse of the economy due to the Civil War
- To ensure that the Red Army was kept supplied with weapons and equipment

Methods

Nationalise all factories

Put all workers' committees under **central control**

End private trade

Force peasants to sell surplus food at a fixed price in order to feed the Red Army and factory workers

Problems

Many factory workers, especially the anarcho-syndicalists, resented central control.

Most peasants objected to the low prices and so began to grow less food and hide any surplus. The government then sent in armed requisition squads to seize the grain.

The disruption caused by the Civil War, and the large areas of important farming land occupied by the Germans, led to **starvation in several parts of Russia by 1921**.

Result

Lenin suggested a change of economic policy, but most Communists rejected this at first.

B The NEP

>> **key fact** Then, in March 1921, came the **Kronstadt Rebellion** in which sailors and workers in Kronstadt, led mainly by left anarchist groups, rose in revolt against War Communism.

* Thousands of rebels and Red Army soldiers died before the rebellion was crushed.

* This revolt led the Communist government to accept Lenin's **New Economic Policy (NEP)** in place of War Communism.

* In **industry**, NEP involved the private sale of some consumer goods and food. Some small factories were returned to former owners or leased out for profit.

* Some left-wing Communists objected so much that they called the NEP the 'New Exploitation of the Proletariat', as they feared it would revive capitalism.

* However, the government kept control of the **commanding heights** of the economy – the banks, railways, heavy industry and foreign trade.

* In **agriculture**, peasants paid their taxes in food and were allowed to sell surplus food for profit – peasants who increased production had their tax reduced. The forcible seizure of grain was stopped.

* By 1924, the NEP had achieved some success – agricultural production had increased, and industry was back to the pre-war production levels of 1913.

* However, some people – **kulaks** (rich peasants) and **nepmen** (private traders) – were becoming very wealthy. This worried many Communists, especially as the Kronstadt Rebellion had shown how isolated the Communists had become by 1921.

remember >>

Because the NEP involved a limited revival of capitalism, the Communist Party decided, as a temporary measure, to ban other parties from the soviets, and factions from within their own party.

>> practice questions

Study Sources A and B below, then answer the question that follows.

	1913	1921	1922	1923	1925	1926
Grain (million tonnes)	80	37	50	57	73	77
Cattle (millions)	59		46		62	
Pigs (millions)	20		12		22	
Coal (million tonnes)	29	9	10	14	18	27
Steel (million tonnes)	4	0.2	0.7	0.7	2	3

Source A: Table of production figures, Russia, 1913–26

There wasn't a scrap of food in the country. We were down to our last small piece of bread per person, then suddenly they announced the NEP. Cafés started opening and factories went back into private hands; it was capitalism. The papers kept quoting Lenin – 'Two steps forward, one step back'; that's all very well but in my eyes what was happening was what I'd struggled against. I can remember the years 1921 and 1922; we used to discuss NEP for hours on end at party meetings. Most people supported Lenin, others said he was wrong; many tore up their party cards.

Source B: An extract from a Bolshevik's memoirs of 1922, about the introduction of the NEP, published in 1987

To what extent do Sources A and B agree that the New Economic Policy was a success?

From Lenin to Stalin

 In 1922, Stalin became General Secretary of the Communist Party.

 Before he died in 1924, Lenin recommended that Stalin be dismissed from all positions of power.

 Eventually, however, Stalin used his position as General Secretary to make himself sole leader of the Communist Party.

A Lenin's 'Last Testament'

1 key fact Part of Stalin's job as General Secretary involved appointing and dismissing party officials, and admitting or expelling members.

- Soon, however, some of his actions began to worry Lenin and other Communists, such as Trotsky. One concern was the **new federal constitution he drew up for the Union of Soviet Socialist Republics (USSR)** – although each national group had its own republic, Stalin gave great powers to central government.

- Then, **in 1922, Lenin suffered the first of several strokes**, which kept him out of active politics for most of the time. Lenin's growing worries led him to turn to Trotsky in an attempt to restore party democracy.

- Although he was popular with the Red Army and ordinary party members, Trotsky had few friends among the party leaders.

- In fact, ever since 1917, there had been serious divisions amongst the party leaders. While Lenin had been active, these had been pushed into the background.

2 key fact Because of his worries, Lenin wrote his 'Last Testament' outlining the strengths and weaknesses of the main Communist leaders. He later added a 'Postscript' that recommended the dismissal of Stalin. Then, in 1924, Lenin died.

- Stalin used jealousies between the party leaders, Trotsky's illness and his powers as General Secretary to stage-manage Lenin's funeral to make it look as though he had been very close to Lenin.

- He then persuaded the party leaders (despite the protests of Lenin's widow) not to act on or publish the 'Last Testament'.

- Stalin was able to do this because of support from Zinoviev and Kamenev. Their position in the party had been weakened by their opposition to Lenin's decision to launch the November Revolution in 1917 – they had even 'leaked' the decision to an opposition newspaper.

- They believed that Stalin's position was so seriously weakened by Lenin's 'Last Testament' that they could use him to block Trotsky.

remember >>

Communists, such as Zinoviev, Kamenev, Bukharin and especially Stalin, resented Trotsky's sudden rise in the party and his closeness to Lenin. Trotsky also became ill during this period.

B The power struggle

>> **key fact** Zinoviev and Kamenev (both more popular than Stalin) thought they could use Stalin to stop Trotsky becoming the new party leader – these three formed a ruling Triumvirate. But this was just the beginning of Stalin's own plans to rise to power, alone.

1

In the **first stage** of Stalin's rise, Stalin sought the **defeat of Trotsky**.

- Pre-1917 disagreements with Lenin were published, and a one-sided debate over policy took place.

- Trotsky continued to defend the policy of **Permanent Revolution**. This had always been party policy and was based on the belief that, because Russia was so backward, it would not be able to become socialist without the help of more economically advanced workers' states.

- Trotsky also argued that the NEP had been as successful ore industrialisation and to begin the collectivisation of agriculture.

- Stalin, however, developed his idea of **Socialism in One Country** – that Russia could achieve socialism on its own. This more conservative and gradual policy appealed to many ordinary party members, who were exhausted after years of struggle and civil war.

- By using his position as General Secretary and the 1921 ban on factions, Stalin got the party to outvote Trotsky and his supporters (known as the **Left Opposition**) and, in 1925, Trotsky was forced to resign as Commissar of War.

2

In the **second stage**, Stalin turned on **Zinoviev** and **Kamenev**, who were beginning to have doubts about Stalin's policies and motives.

- When they formed the **United Left Opposition** with Trotsky, Stalin accused them of 'Trotskyism'.

- Supported by the **Centre and Right** of the party, Stalin got them expelled in 1927.

3

In the **final stage**, Stalin defeated the **Right**, which was led by **Bukharin**.

- In 1928, Stalin suddenly decided to end the NEP, but Bukharin and the Right disagreed. Stalin began to dismiss Bukharin's supporters and, in desperation, Bukharin turned to Trotsky in an attempt to restore democracy.

- But it was too late – Bukharin was defeated in 1929, and Trotsky was expelled from the USSR. This left Stalin as sole leader of the Communist Party.

> **remember >>**
>
> Lenin and other leaders, as well as Trotsky, had always argued that it was necessary to help workers' revolutions throughout the world. 'Permanent Revolution' would also mean ending the NEP.

>> practice questions

1 Which three leading Communists made up the 'Triumvirate'?

2 How did Stalin's job as General Secretary help him defeat all his opponents?

Stalin's revolution

- By 1928, Stalin had decided to modernise Soviet industry, but this required a more efficient agricultural system.

- A serious food shortage in 1928 led Stalin to end the NEP and to begin forced (compulsory) collectivisation of agriculture instead.

- At the same time, Stalin decided on a series of Five-Year Plans to bring about rapid industrialisation.

- By 1940, the USSR was the world's second largest industrial producer, after the USA.

A Collectivisation

1 key fact In the late 1920s, most farms were very small and used old-fashioned methods. Many poorer peasants had no land at all.

- Stalin's industrialisation plans meant peasants had to produce more food in order to feed the extra factory workers required, and that the USSR had to buy more advanced foreign machinery with the money raised from grain exports.

- In 1927, peasants were encouraged to join their plots together to form larger **state collective farms (kolkhozes)** that would be more efficient, but few did.

- A serious food shortage in 1928 led Stalin to begin **forced (compulsory) collectivisation**.

2 key fact Most of the land given to the peasants in 1917 became state collectives, with peasants only being allowed small private plots.

- The government set up **Motor Tractor Stations (MTS)** to provide tractors and other modern machinery to make collectives more efficient.

- However, there was **much opposition**, especially **from the kulaks**. Many slaughtered their animals and destroyed crops and machinery rather than turn them over to the collectives. They even attacked and killed Communist officials.

> **remember >>**
>
> It was not until 1941 that food production levels returned to those of 1928.

3 key fact Stalin then resorted to harsh measures – many kulaks were hanged and many more were sent to poor farming areas or to the gulags (prison work camps). Those who remained were reluctant to work hard.

- Food production dropped sharply, so the government sent **armed detachments** into the countryside to collect food for the towns.

- In some rural areas, several million people died from **famine**.

B The Five-Year Plans

① key fact Despite the successes of the NEP, Soviet industry was limited in 1928.

- Stalin decided on rapid industrialisation as he feared invasion by capitalist nations. All factories that had been privately owned under the NEP were re-nationalised.

- Stalin also saw industrialisation as a way to **make the USSR more socialist**.

- The **State Planning Commission (Gosplan)** drew up a **Five-Year Plan** that set targets for increased production for each industry.

② key fact Stalin launched three Five-Year Plans between 1928 and 1941.

The First Five-Year Plan, 1928–32, concentrated on **heavy industry** (coal, iron, steel, oil and electricity).	**The Second Five-Year Plan, 1932–7, was similar to the first, but also developed transport and mining.**	**The Third Five-Year Plan**, which began in 1938, put more emphasis on **light industry, housing and consumer goods** (but later switched to war production because of the growing threat from Nazi Germany).

- Despite official exaggeration and the failure to meet some targets, these Five-Year Plans were very successful.

- Many new industries and industrial centres were built, and most workers benefited from the lack of unemployment and the provision of free health care and education.

C Methods

Skilled foreign workers were employed to teach new techniques.

Methods to increase production

Women and peasants were encouraged to work in factories. Free crèches and canteens made it easier for women to work.

Workers who exceeded their work 'norms' received extra pay, various privileges and medals – these 'super' workers were known as 'Stakhanovites', after the miner Stakhanov, who had greatly increased his output.

Harsh methods were used – hours of work were increased, fines for lateness were imposed, and many were sent to the gulags, where they had to work in poor conditions.

>> practice questions

1 What do you understand by the term 'heavy industry'?

2 List three ways in which Stalin helped to ensure the success of the Five-Year Plans.

The approach of war

- Although Stalin had defeated all his rivals by 1929, he still feared opposition.

- Stalin's security concerns increased after 1933, when Hitler came to power in Germany.

- To ensure his position, even in the event of war, Stalin launched the Great Purge and Terror.

- He also decided to sign a non-aggression pact with Germany in August 1939, in order to gain time to build up Soviet defences.

A   The Great Purge and Terror

① key fact Even Stalin's supporters were reluctant to expel leading Communists. Some also criticised his policy of forced collectivisation.

- So Stalin expanded the secret police (renamed **NKVD** in 1934) to spy on possible critics.

- In 1934, **Kirov** (party boss in Leningrad) was assassinated – he had been very popular at the Seventeenth Party Congress earlier that year.

② key fact Stalin used Kirov's death as an excuse to launch what became known as the Great Purge and Terror.

remember >>
Statues and posters of Stalin appeared everywhere, and films and books praised his actions. He also took control of the Komsomol (Young Communist League).

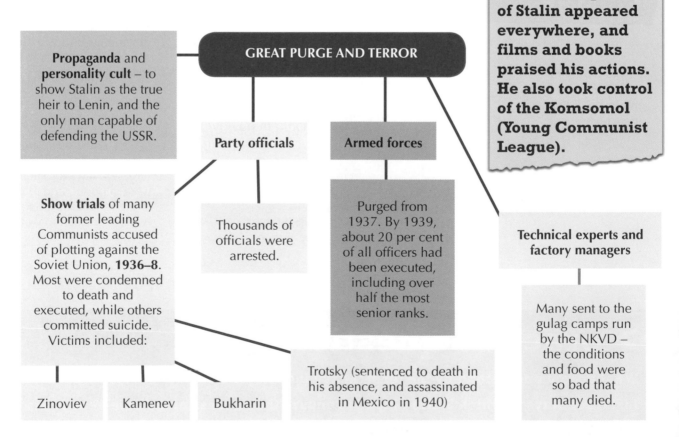

GREAT PURGE AND TERROR

Propaganda and **personality cult** – to show Stalin as the true heir to Lenin, and the only man capable of defending the USSR.

Party officials

Armed forces

Show trials of many former leading Communists accused of plotting against the Soviet Union, **1936–8**. Most were condemned to death and executed, while others committed suicide. Victims included:

Thousands of officials were arrested.

Purged from 1937. By 1939, about 20 per cent of all officers had been executed, including over half the most senior ranks.

Technical experts and factory managers

Many sent to the gulag camps run by the NKVD – the conditions and food were so bad that many died.

Zinoviev   Kamenev   Bukharin

Trotsky (sentenced to death in his absence, and assassinated in Mexico in 1940)

B Foreign policy

① key fact
After the November Revolution in 1917, fourteen different countries had intervened in the Civil War on the side of the Whites.

- In 1919, in an attempt to help spread world revolution and end Russia's isolation, the Communists had set up the **Communist International (Comintern)**.

- However, under Stalin and his policy of Socialism in One Country, the Comintern declined in importance.

② key fact
After the Wall Street Crash in 1929, Stalin feared European capitalist countries might try to solve their problems by invading the USSR.

remember >>
The Nazi–Soviet pact contained secret clauses to divide Poland between the two countries – this would give the USSR a buffer zone when the expected Nazi attack came, and would allow time for building up the USSR's defences.

In 1932, he signed a **non-aggression pact with France**. **Japanese aggression in the Far East** against China was another concern.

Stalin became increasingly worried after 1933, because Hitler made no secret of his plan to take '**living space**' for Germany from Eastern Europe – especially from the USSR.

Stalin – in view of Britain and France's continued refusal to sign an anti-Nazi agreement – then decided to buy extra time for the USSR by signing a **non-aggression (Ribbentrop–Molotov) pact with Germany in August 1939**.

However, Stalin became alarmed at Britain and France's policy of **appeasing** Hitler's demands and at Hitler's breaches of the Treaty of Versailles, especially after the **Czech crisis over the Sudetenland in 1938**.

At first, Stalin tried to secure agreements with Britain and France, and the USSR was allowed to join the League of Nations in 1934. The Comintern was ordered to form **popular fronts** with all those opposed to Fascism.

>> practice questions

Study Source A, then answer the questions that follow.

1 What crisis of 1938 finally led Stalin to sign a non-aggression pact with Nazi Germany in 1939?

2 Explain how the secret clause about the division of Poland in this pact supposed to help Stalin defend the USSR.

Source A: Soviet cartoon showing Britain and France directing Hitler and the Nazis to go east to the USSR ('CCCP'), and not towards Western Europe

Changes in Germany

 By 1918, Germany was in a desperate state, on the verge of defeat and revolution.

 When the Kaiser fled and abdicated, a new democratic provisional government agreed to sign an armistice with the Allies.

 Eventually, a new constitution (known as the Weimar Constitution) gave the German people full democracy for the first time.

A Impact of the First World War

1 key fact By 1918, the German army was near defeat. The Allied naval blockade was creating near-starvation conditions, there were serious fuel shortages and the country was in financial ruin.

In October 1918, sailors at Kiel naval base mutinied. Soon, workers and soldiers in Kiel and elsewhere began to form councils and soviets.

As mutinies and uprisings spread across Germany, the Kaiser – who still refused to share power with the Reichstag (German parliament) – fled and abdicated.

Once he had gone, a centre-left coalition provisional government was set up under the leadership of Ebert, a leading member of the Social Democratic Party (SPD).

Ebert declared Germany a democratic republic, agreed to sign an armistice with the Allies, and arranged for elections in January 1919.

2 key fact However, in Berlin, the revolutionary socialists of the Spartacist League tried to start a workers' revolution similar to the one that had taken place in Russia in November 1917.

Ebert, under pressure from army leaders, agreed to call in the army to crush this **Spartacist Revolt** – a paramilitary group of unemployed right-wing soldiers (**the Freikorps**) were also used to put down the rising.

Thousands of workers were killed during the suppression, including the leaders, **Karl Liebnechkt** and **Rosa Luxembourg**, who were captured and then murdered.

> **remember >>**
>
> The Spartacists who survived later formed the German Communist Party (KPD).

B Establishment of the Weimar Republic

1 **key fact** Germany from 1919 to 1933 is usually referred to as the Weimar Republic or Weimar Germany. This is because the Spartacist Revolt of 1919 and its suppression in Berlin forced the provisional government to move to Weimar to draw up a new democratic constitution for Germany.

- The new Weimar Constitution gave the vote to all people over the age of 20, and used a system of **proportional representation (PR)** for elections to the **Reichstag** (parliament).

- Elections were to take place every four years, and governments – headed by a Chancellor (Prime Minister) – were chosen from, and were responsible to, the Reichstag.

- Germany became a federal system, with power shared between central government and **eighteen new Lander (state) governments**.

> **remember >>**
>
> The Weimar Constitution had a Fundamental Rights section that guaranteed freedom of speech, religious belief and travel.

2 **key fact** Article 48 of the constitution gave the President emergency powers to rule by decree without the Reichstag, and even to suspend the constitution. The President was to be directly elected every seven years.

- Due to PR, there were many small parties in the Reichstag, so most Weimar governments were often short-lived **coalitions**. From 1919 to 1923, Germany had nine coalition governments – these often found it difficult to agree on policies.

- This was at a time when many Germans were bitterly angry at the Treaty of Versailles – many blamed the new government for signing it, and referred to them as the **November Criminals** who had 'stabbed Germany in the back'.

>> practice questions

Study Source A below, then answer the questions that follow.

	1919	1920	1924 May	1924 Dec	1928
German Communist Party (KPD)	–	2	12	9	11
Social Democratic Party (SPD)	38	21	21	26	30
German Democratic Party (DDP)	19	8	6	6	5
Centre Party	20	18	17	18	15
German People's Party (DVP)	4	14	9	10	9
German Nationalists Party (DNVP)	10	15	19	21	14
Nazi Party (NSDAP)	–	–	7	3	2
Other (minor) parties	9	22	9	7	14

(% of votes won)

Source A: Results of the elections in Germany, 1919–28

1 Which three parties, according to this source, tended to dominate elections in Weimar Germany during the period 1919–28?

2 What can you learn from the election results about politics in Weimar Germany?

Weimar Germany, 1919–23

- The new Weimar Republic faced many problems in this period.

- There was much violent political opposition. In 1920, a new right-wing party – the Nazi Party – was founded.

- There were also serious economic problems, connected to the war and reparations, which brought the German economy near to collapse by 1920.

A Early problems

1 key fact Many Germans hated the new government for signing the armistice and the Treaty of Versailles. Many preferred the authoritarian rule of the Kaiser – they saw democracy as a foreign idea imposed on Germany by the Allies.

LEFT	RIGHT
• The new **Communist Party (KPD)** organised strikes in Berlin in March 1919 that were suppressed by the army and the Freikorps. • There was an unsuccessful Communist uprising in Munich in which the army shot many workers. • A **Communist uprising in the Ruhr**, following Kapp's Putsch of 1920, was bloodily suppressed by the army and Freikorps, who shot over 2000 workers.	• **Extreme nationalist groups** murdered numerous left-wing and liberal politicians in the years 1920–3. • In March 1920, the army made no effort to stop **Kapp's Putsch** (an attempted Freikorps coup against the government). Instead, it was defeated by a general strike organised by the workers of Berlin.

Opposition to the Weimar Republic

2 key fact In 1922, Germany said it could not afford to pay its second reparations instalment.

So, **in 1923, French and Belgian troops occupied the Ruhr**, Germany's richest industrial area, in order to take food, coal, iron ore and steel as payment.

Germany replied with **passive resistance** (strikes and non-cooperation). The French deported 150 000 strikers and 132 Germans were killed in separate incidents.

The German economy collapsed, leading to **hyper-inflation** (massive, rapid price increases), which even began to affect France.

A new German government, led by **Stresemann**, ended passive resistance, and the French finally withdrew.

remember >>

Most of the civil servants, judges and army and police officers who had served under the Kaiser kept their jobs after 1918. But many were opposed to the democracy of the Weimar Constitution.

B The birth of the Nazi Party

① key fact In 1920, the NSDAP (Nazi Party) was formed and, in 1921, Adolf Hitler became its leader.

- Two years before, in 1919, Hitler (an Austrian who had fought in the German army) had been sent by the army to Munich to spy on the small **German Workers' Party (DAP)**, which they thought might be a left-wing party.

- In fact, it was an extreme nationalist party, and Hitler decided to join it. In 1920, he persuaded it to change its name to the National Socialist German Workers' Party (NSDAP), and to adopt a **25-point programme** that contained nationalist and anti-Semitic (anti-Jewish) policies, with some vague socialist elements.

- In 1921, Hitler became party leader and the Nazi Party adopted the **swastika** as its emblem.

- Hitler set up the **Stormtroopers (SA)**. These **Brownshirts** (so-called because of their uniform) were mainly ex-soldiers, who attacked left-wing political meetings and demonstrations.

- The Nazis soon had over 50 000 members in southern Germany, and received donations from various sources, including the army.

② key fact When the German government called off passive resistance against the French occupation of the Ruhr in September 1923, German nationalists were furious. Hitler decided to march to Berlin to overthrow the Weimar government.

- In November 1923, the Nazis took over a beer hall where important Bavarian officials were addressing a meeting. Hitler tried unsuccessfully to get their support for his **March on Berlin**.

- However, Hitler, supported by General Ludendorff (a First World War leader), went ahead with his plans. But his **Beer Hall Putsch** collapsed when the march was stopped by armed police. In the fighting, one policeman and sixteen Nazis were killed. Hitler ran away but was later arrested.

- Hitler was accused of treason, but the Munich judges allowed him to make long speeches at his trial, which were widely reported across Germany by sympathetic newspapers.

- Hitler was given the lightest possible sentence – five years in Landsberg Prison.

> **remember >>**
>
> Hitler was a powerful public speaker. He blamed all Germany's problems on Weimar, Communists and Jews.

>> practice questions

1 Why did France and Belgium occupy the Ruhr in January 1923?

2 What was the hyperinflation of 1923?

Germany before the Depression

- The 1923 hyperinflation in Germany caused great hardship for many people.

- In September 1923, Gustav Stresemann became Chancellor. Under him, Germany began to prosper in what became known as the 'Golden Years'.

- Stresemann's economic and diplomatic achievements meant that more extreme parties did badly in elections. For the Nazi Party, the years 1924–9 became known as their 'Lean Years'.

A Stresemann and the 'Golden Years'

>> **key fact** By the time Stresemann became Chancellor in September 1923, many Germans were suffering greatly from the effects of hyperinflation, especially those with savings or on fixed incomes (e.g. pensions).

Hyperinflation → Money had become so worthless that workers had to be paid twice a day so items could be bought before prices went up again. → Stresemann called off passive resistance and **promised to pay reparations**.

German industry began to revive. Unemployment fell. Stresemann then began to restore Germany's position by co-operating with the Allies. ← In November 1923, Stresemann introduced a **new currency (Rentenmark)** to end inflation.

In 1924, Stresemann negotiated the **Dawes Plan** with the USA. This **reduced the size of reparation instalments** and provided Germany with **US loans** that were used to modernise factories and build new ones. → In 1929, the **Young Plan** brought **more loans**, while reparations were reduced and spread over sixty years. → Between 1924 and 1929, Germany received over 25 billion gold marks in loans – three times more than reparation payments. By 1929, Germany was second only to the USA in advanced industrial production.

---

remember >>

In the Locarno Treaty of 1925, Germany accepted its 1919 western frontiers, and agreed that changes in the east would be by negotiation only.

remember >>

Germany joined the League of Nations in 1926.

remember >>

The Kellogg-Briand Pact of 1928 saw Germany, along with 44 other countries, renounce war.

B The Nazis' 'Lean Years'

① key fact During the period 1924–9, Stresemann's policies achieved some of the changes demanded by the right.

- As a result, **support for extreme parties declined.**
- Although Hitler had been sentenced to five years for his part in the **Beer Hall Putsch**, he was released in December 1924 after serving only nine months.

② key fact When Hitler came out of prison, he found Germany much improved and, while he had been inside, the Nazi Party had been banned, had split into factions, and membership had dropped.

- As a result, the Nazis did badly in elections in the period 1924–30, which is known as **the Nazi Party's Lean Years.**
- Hitler reorganised the party. It was relaunched in 1925, and power was concentrated in Hitler's hands. Special sections (for students, teachers, farmers, and the Hitler Youth for young people) were set up to recruit more members, and party branches were founded all over Germany.
- **In 1926, Goebbels took control of Nazi Party propaganda.** By 1928, the Nazis had just over 100 000 members.

③ key fact Hitler also decided that to win power the Nazis would have to use elections.

- The experience of the Beer Hall Putsch convinced Hitler of the **need to win over the army and wealthy industrialists.**
- However, Hitler had no intention of abandoning violence; in 1925, he set up the **black-shirted SS (Schutz Staffel).**
- Officially, this was his personal bodyguard, but it soon increased in size and attacked opponents. **In 1929, Himmler became its head.**

>> practice questions

Study Source A below, then answer the questions that follow.

> When I resume active work, it will be necessary to pursue a new policy. Instead of working to achieve power by an armed coup, we will have to hold our noses and enter the Reichstag against the Catholic and Marxist members. If outvoting them takes longer than outshooting them, at least the result will be guaranteed by their own constitution. Any lawful process is slow. Sooner or later we will have a majority, and, after that – Germany!

Source A: An extract from a letter written by Hitler in 1923 while he was in Landsberg Prison

1 Why, by 1923, did Hitler think that he had to change his tactics for gaining power?

2 Briefly explain how Hitler reorganised the Nazi Party in the years 1925–9.

The Nazis come to power

- The Great Depression, which began in 1929, soon affected Germany badly; coalition governments were often short-lived.

- The Nazis gained popular support and, by 1932, were the largest single party. In January 1933, Hitler became Chancellor.

- By 1934, Germany was under Nazi control.

A Depression and the rise of the Nazis

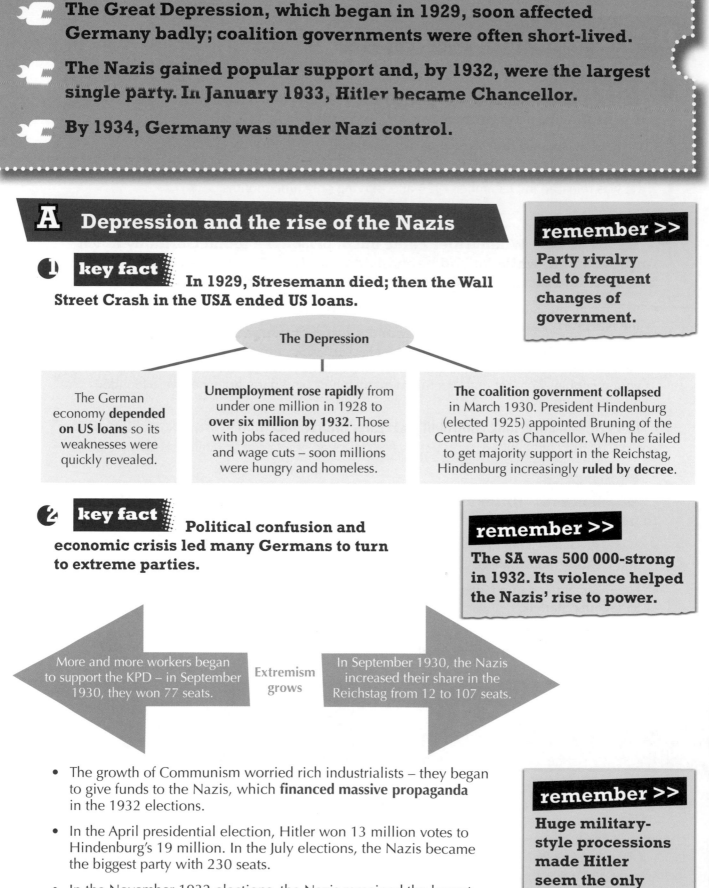

(1) key fact In 1929, Stresemann died; then the Wall Street Crash in the USA ended US loans.

remember >>
Party rivalry led to frequent changes of government.

The Depression

The German economy **depended on US loans** so its weaknesses were quickly revealed.

Unemployment rose rapidly from under one million in 1928 to **over six million by 1932**. Those with jobs faced reduced hours and wage cuts – soon millions were hungry and homeless.

The coalition government collapsed in March 1930. President Hindenburg (elected 1925) appointed Bruning of the Centre Party as Chancellor. When he failed to get majority support in the Reichstag, Hindenburg increasingly **ruled by decree**.

(2) key fact Political confusion and economic crisis led many Germans to turn to extreme parties.

remember >>
The SA was 500 000-strong in 1932. Its violence helped the Nazis' rise to power.

More and more workers began to support the KPD – in September 1930, they won 77 seats.

Extremism grows

In September 1930, the Nazis increased their share in the Reichstag from 12 to 107 seats.

- The growth of Communism worried rich industrialists – they began to give funds to the Nazis, which **financed massive propaganda** in the 1932 elections.

- In the April presidential election, Hitler won 13 million votes to Hindenburg's 19 million. In the July elections, the Nazis became the biggest party with 230 seats.

- In the November 1932 elections, the Nazis remained the largest party but lost 34 seats, while the Communists rose again.

- In January 1933, von Papen (leader of the Nationalists) persuaded Hindenburg to appoint Hitler as Chancellor of a Nationalist-dominated coalition government.

remember >>
Huge military-style processions made Hitler seem the only man capable of restoring order.

B Establishing the Nazi dictatorship

key fact Although there were only three Nazi ministers in Hitler's government, he planned to take complete power.

- Hitler called a new election for March 1933, and SA and SS violence increased.

- In February, just before the elections, the **Reichstag Fire** took place – the Nazis blamed the Communists, whose leaders and candidates were quickly rounded up.

- In Prussia (the largest Land, or state), the Minister of the Interior was **Goring**, a leading Nazi. He enrolled SA members into the police – over 4000 KPD and SPD members were arrested, their meetings broken up and their newspapers banned.

- The Nazis failed to get an overall majority in the Reichstag, despite banning those Communists who had managed to get elected. **The Nationalists then agreed to support the Nazis – this gave Hitler control.**

key fact By intimidating or excluding SPD deputies, Hitler got the Reichstag to pass the Enabling Act in March 1933.

- Hindenburg agreed to suspend the constitution and give Hitler the **power to rule by decree for four years**. Hitler then moved quickly to destroy Weimar democracy.

- In April, all eighteen Lander were taken over by Nazi gauleiters (regional party officials). In May, **trade unions were banned**, and in July **all opposition parties were banned** (or persuaded to disband) and **Germany became a one-party dictatorship**. By then, most KPD and SPD leaders and activists were in **concentration camps run by the SA**.

key fact Hitler also faced opposition from the more militant wing of the SA, including its leader Ernst Rohm.

- Among other demands, the SA wanted to become the new German army. However, the army officers and the industrialists opposed this.

- In June 1934, Hitler ordered the **Night of the Long Knives**, in which the SS (with army help) murdered Rohm and other SA leaders.

- This reassured the generals and, when Hindenburg died in August, **they supported Hitler becoming Führer of Germany** – Hitler was now President, Chancellor and Commander-in-Chief (C-in-C) of the armed forces.

> **remember >>**
>
> Militants in the SA wanted Hitler to carry out the party's left-wing promises.

>> practice questions

1. What problems did Hitler have with Ernst Rohm and the more militant sections of the SA?

2. What happened after the Night of the Long Knives?

Maintaining Nazi control

- Once established in power, the Nazi dictatorship was maintained by a constant campaign of terror and propaganda.

- Nazi control was also maintained by economic and social policies.

A Terror and propaganda

① key fact The terror campaign was carried out by the Gestapo (secret police) and the SS (which, by 1935, had grown to over 200 000). Both were controlled by Himmler.

remember >>
At first, concentration camps were mainly for political prisoners.

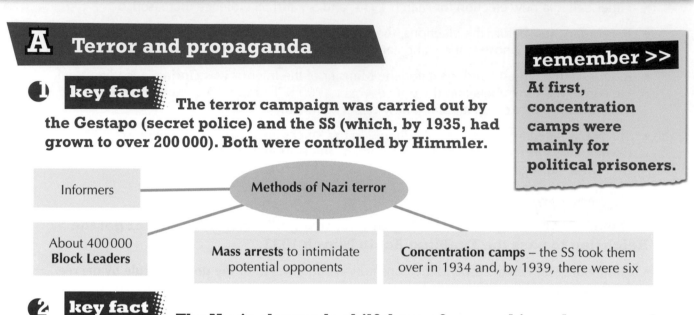

Informers

About 400 000 **Block Leaders**

Methods of Nazi terror

Mass arrests to intimidate potential opponents

Concentration camps – the SS took them over in 1934 and, by 1939, there were six

② key fact The Nazis also made skilful use of censorship and propaganda directed by Goebbels, Minister of Propaganda and Culture.

Newspapers were banned or censored.

Cheap radios were produced.

Nazi censorship and propaganda

The Nazis' massive **Nuremberg rallies** were filmed for the cinema, which also reflected Nazi ideology.

Loudspeakers were placed in all workplaces and public areas to ensure everyone heard Nazi views.

Works of literature and art that conflicted with Nazi ideas were outlawed and destroyed.

B Nazi economic and social policies

remember >>
Communists, Jews, women forced out of jobs and those in camps were not counted as unemployed.

① key fact In order to achieve his foreign policy aims, Hitler knew he needed to reduce unemployment and strengthen the German economy, so that Germany could rearm and be self-sufficient. The Nazis dealt with unemployment in several ways.

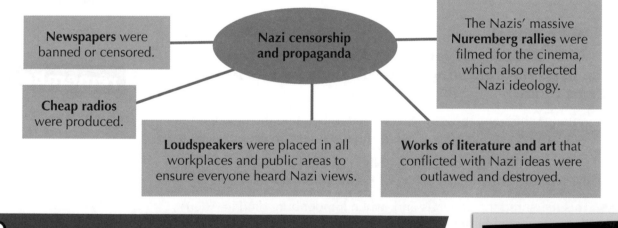

Public works, funded by government money, gave work to the unemployed. The main projects were building houses, hospitals, schools and, especially, roads (to allow quick movement of troops) and barracks. By 1939, unemployment had fallen to 100 000.

The **National Labour Service** (set up before 1933) was expanded. From 1935, it was compulsory for all men aged 18–25 for six months.

When trade unions were abolished in 1933, all workers had to join the Nazis' **German Labour Front**. Strikes were illegal, wages remained low, even after full employment, and the working day became longer.

To keep workers happy, various schemes (such as **Strength Through Joy**) provided cheap holidays and leisure activities.

② key fact — Rearmament began in 1933 in secret, but, by 1935, was carried out openly.

- **Rearmament** and **conscription** gave employment to many. The drive for **self-sufficiency** also created new jobs.

- Under **Schacht**, Minister of the Economy, agricultural production was increased and imports were reduced (partly by finding substitutes for foreign goods).

- In 1936, Goring was ordered to get Germany ready for war, by preparing a **Four-Year Plan**.

- Goring's Four-Year Plan undermined Schacht's work, so Schacht resigned in 1937.

③ key fact — The Nazis also tried to control women and young people, to make sure they played a part in creating an Aryan society.

Policies were based on the **3 Ks (Kinder, Kirche, Küche)**. Women were encouraged by a system of loans to stay at home and have children.

The **Motherhood Cross** system gave medals to women who had large families.

The Nazis wanted to control **young people** to ensure support in the future.

All teachers had to swear loyalty to Hitler and join the Nazi **Teacher's League**. A new national curriculum was drawn up and centrally imposed.

Nazi policies for women

Nazi policies for young people

To make sure they stayed at home, **laws forced women out of various state and professional jobs** and **employers were encouraged to give all jobs to men**.

Most advances towards equal rights and opportunities for women under the Weimar Republic were removed.

Great emphasis was placed on: **history** (to show the 'greatness' of the Nazis); **biology** (to teach 'race science', which stressed the superiority of Aryans); and **PE** (to get boys fit for the army and girls fit to be mothers).

Out of school, young people were encouraged to join the **Hitler Youth** movements. **In 1939, membership became compulsory.**

>> practice questions

1 **How did the lives of women change under the Nazis?**

2 **Why were the Nazis so concerned about controlling young people?**

Outside the Nazi 'community'

- While many people supported Nazi policies, others remained excluded from the Nazis' 'national people's community' (*Volksgemeinschaft*), especially the Jews.

- Some people who opposed the Nazis continued to resist after 1933, despite the risks.

A Jewish people

1 key fact The Nazis were racist and believed all non-Aryan groups were inferior – Jews, Blacks, Slavs and gypsies (Sinti and Roma). They wanted to create a pure Aryan 'master race'.

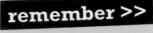

remember >>

Another five million 'racially inferior' people were murdered by SS 'Special Action' groups and in the extermination camps – mainly homosexuals, Slavs and gypsies.

In April 1933, Hitler ordered the SA and SS to organise a **boycott of Jewish shops**. However, this received little popular support and was quickly dropped.

In 1934, Jews were **banned from public facilities** such as parks and swimming pools.

In 1935, the Nuremberg Laws deprived all Jews of German Citizenship, and forbade inter-marriage. After 1936, other laws further restricted the rights of Jews to work and own property.

The main victims of Nazi racism – Jewish people

Laws were passed to sack Jews from the civil service, the law and education.

In November 1938, Kristallnacht (Night of Broken Glass) saw attacks on Jewish homes, shops and synagogues after a Nazi diplomat was assassinated by a Jew in Paris. About 100 Jews were killed, and over 20 000 were put in concentration camps. After a week of terror, the Nazis fined the Jews one billion marks.

2 key fact After the Second World War began in 1939, Nazi action became even more extreme. To start with, all Jews in areas invaded by the Nazis were forced to live in ghettos.

In the summer of 1941, Himmler ordered SS **Special Action Groups** to kill all Soviet Jews.

Then, at the **Wannsee Conference, January 1942**, leading Nazis decided to exterminate all Jews in Europe – the **Final Solution** – with Adolf Eichmann in charge of overall planning.

Extermination camps (for example, Auschwitz) were built in Eastern Europe. About six million Jews died in the **Holocaust**.

B Opposition

① key fact In March 1933, even after intimidation and violence, the Nazis had only been able to win 43 per cent of the vote. There were many who continued to oppose Hitler's regime after 1933 despite Nazi propaganda and terror – even though most of them lost their lives doing so.

remember >>

Religious groups also put up some opposition – for example, Hitler was forced to drop his euthanasia programme because of protests from the churches.

University students in Munich formed the **White Rose Group** – they distributed leaflets, wrote anti-Nazi slogans on walls and even organised demonstrations. Their leaders were guillotined in 1944.

Communists and Social Democrats set up underground organisations – these published anti-Nazi leaflets and organised industrial sabotage and strikes. The Communist Red Orchestra (Rote Kapelle) group also passed on military secrets to the Soviet Union until they were betrayed and arrested by the Gestapo.

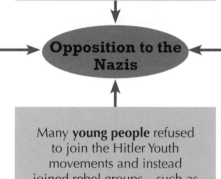

Opposition to the Nazis

Opposition in the **army**, especially the Beck–Goerdeler group, increased as the war began to go badly. Colonel von Stauffenberg led the **July Bomb Plot in 1944**, which only just failed to assassinate Hitler.

Many **young people** refused to join the Hitler Youth movements and instead joined rebel groups – such as **the Swing, the Meuten or the Eidelweiss Pirates**.

② key fact Opposition also began to emerge amongst members of the elite, who had at first supported the Nazis.

>> practice questions

Study Source A, then answer the questions that follow.

1 How useful is this source as evidence the treatment of Jewish people in Nazi Germany in the years 1933–9?

2 Apart from the boycott of 1933, shown in Source A, what other actions were taken against Jewish people before 1939?

Source A: SA and SS men enforcing a boycott of Jewish shops, 1933

The Republican era begins

- When the First World War ended in 1918, in which 100 000 US soldiers had died, US President Wilson (Democrat) wanted the USA to continue its involvement with Europe.

- But many Americans, including some Democrats, wanted the USA to return to its traditional policy of 'isolationism'.

- By 1918, the USA had become the world's most powerful and wealthy industrial country – this formed the basis for an economic 'boom' in the 1920s.

A Isolationism

① key fact Woodrow Wilson's plans to continue US involvement in Europe failed because so many wanted to return to 'isolationism' (staying out of foreign alliances and avoiding close involvement in European affairs).

- The US Congress had been dominated by the **Republicans** since the 1918 mid-term elections.

- Despite Wilson's efforts, Congress refused to sign the Treaty of Versailles or join the League of Nations.

② key fact By 1919, many Americans saw the 'Old World' of Europe as being full of poverty, oppression and dangerous revolutionary ideas and movements (such as socialism, Communism and anarchism).

Before 1919, most immigrants to the USA had been **White Anglo-Saxon Protestants (WASPs)** from the more prosperous parts of Northern and Western Europe.

After 1919, most immigrants came from the poorer parts of Southern and Eastern Europe – where there were many Catholics, and where many revolutionary outbreaks took place in the years 1917–20.

The result was **increasing restrictions on immigration** – these included the imposition of a **literacy test** in 1917 and of **limits and quotas in 1921, 1924 and 1929.**

Between 1920 and 1929, immigration fell from 850 000 a year to 150 000.

remember >>

Wilson had drawn up his Fourteen Points as the basis for peace in 1918.

remember >>

There were two main parties in the USA – the Republicans and the Democrats.

B   The Republican 'boom'

① **key fact** The USA had stayed out of the First World War until 1917, and during that time had taken much trade from European nations such as Britain and Germany.

remember >>

This economic boom was helped by mass production, radio advertising and hire purchase (HP).

- US companies had also made huge profits **selling weapons** to the Allies, while **US banks had loaned money**.

- At the end of the war, these profits were invested in **new industries** (chemicals, cars, radios, the telephone, electrical goods).

- By 1918, the USA was the **wealthiest and most powerful industrial country in the world**, with **plenty of raw materials** (wood, coal, iron, oil).

② **key fact** Republican presidents, who were in power throughout the 'boom' years, believed in 'laissez-faire' economics.

- Wilson had placed restrictions on US companies to protect the public and especially the less well-off. The Republicans immediately lifted these restrictions, and cut taxes for the rich.

- Instead, the huge **trusts** (large firms) were allowed to do as they wanted and **tariffs** (customs duties) were imposed on European goods (e.g. **Fordney-McCumber Act, 1922**). This was known as **protectionism**.

③ **key fact** Some new industries, such as car manufacturing, led to increased demand for steel, leather, glass, rubber and roads.

- The US economy experienced a boom (the 1920s were known as the **Jazz Age**). For the first time, the majority of Americans lived in **urban areas**.

- However, **many rural areas missed out on the prosperity** of the 1920s, as did some groups of people (African-Americans, the poor and some farmers).

>> practice questions

Study Source A, then answer the question that follows.

exam tip >>

Remember to use details from the source and your knowledge to explain your answer – and try to comment on the possible purpose of the source.

How far do you trust this source as evidence of the prosperity of the USA in the 1920s, before the end of the Republican 'boom'?

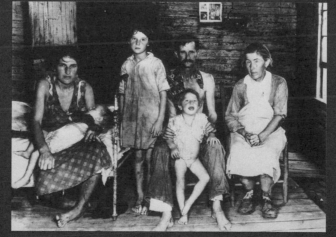

Source A: An American family in the 1920s

Problems during the boom

 In 1918, the prohibition of alcohol in the USA began a 15-year period of organised crime, corruption and violence, before Prohibition was finally ended.

 Another serious problem in the USA during the 1920s was racial and political intolerance, which was often violent.

A Prohibition and gangsters

1 key fact In 1918, women in the Anti-Saloon League and the Women's Christian Temperance Union succeeded in getting Congress to add the Eighteenth Amendment to the US Constitution.

- This was known as **Prohibition** and made the sale, production and transport of alcohol illegal. The **Volstead Act** then made buying alcohol illegal, too.

- The groups (mainly rural) behind Prohibition had pushed for these changes to avoid the problems associated with excessive alcohol consumption – poverty, absence from work, public drunkenness, violence in the home and on the streets and crime.

2 key fact However, these developments gave new opportunities for organised crime.

- This was because many US citizens were prepared to break these laws in order to continue drinking alcohol. This resulted in **speakeasies** (illegal bars), **moonshine** (spirits made and sold illegally) and **bootlegging** (smuggling alcohol).

- Prohibition helped lead to the emergence of **gangsters such as Al Capone and 'Bugs' Moran**.

- These gangs became so wealthy from supplying illegal alcohol that they were able to get involved in other crimes too (prostitution, protection, gambling).

- They then used this wealth to **bribe police, judges and local politicians**.

- There were also gun battles between gangsters and the police.

- Al Capone became so wealthy and powerful, he even controlled the Mayor of Chicago, and was able to 'run' Chicago for several years.

- As rival gangs fought to control areas, there was a big increase in gang murders – the worst case was the **St Valentine's Day Massacre** in Chicago in 1929. This was when Capone ordered the killing of members of the rival gang run by 'Bugs' Moran.

- This increase in crime and corruption worried many. **In 1933, the Twenty-First Amendment** ended Prohibition.

> **remember >>**
>
> Capone's income was probably more than $27 million a year. He was finally imprisoned in 1931 for tax evasion.

B Intolerance in the USA

1 **key fact** African-Americans suffered most from intolerance during the 1920s, as well as benefiting the least from the boom.

- By 1920, there were 12 million African-Americans (about 10 per cent of the population), of whom 75 per cent lived in the Southern states, where they experienced poverty and discrimination.

- Despite being freed from slavery in 1865, the **Jim Crow** laws in the Southern states imposed segregation and prevented most African-Americans from voting (for example, by setting literacy tests that were not given to poor whites).

- In addition, African-Americans suffered from **Ku Klux Klan (KKK)** violence, which included burnings, beatings and lynchings.

- By 1925, the KKK had almost five million (WASP) members and many more sympathisers, **including many law officials**.

- During the 1920s, over 1.5 million African-Americans left the South for Northern cities. However, although there were better opportunities in the North, as there was no segregation, they still experienced discrimination (housing, jobs and wages). There was also racial hostility and violence in some areas.

> **remember >>**
>
> The KKK (a white supremacist and anti-Black group set up in the South after the Civil War) was revived in 1915. The KKK also had a fanatical hatred of Catholics, Jews, socialists and Communists.

2 **key fact** Left-wingers and radicals were victims of a Red Scare during the 1920s, begun by powerful Americans who were opposed to socialism, Communism and anarchism.

- Left-wingers were harassed by the police, and even deported from the USA by the Federal Justice Department.

- **Wealthy industrialists, such as Henry Ford**, refused to allow their workers to join trade unions, and even employed thugs against trade unionists and strikers. Not surprisingly, trade union membership dropped from 5 million to 3 million during the 1920s.

- The most serious example of this intolerance was the case of two Italian anarchists, **Sacco and Vanzetti, who were executed in 1927**.

- Because they 'admitted' to being anarchists, their trial was more about their revolutionary views than the weak evidence presented by the police in an attempt to link them to a serious crime.

- Although 107 witnesses swore on oath that the two men had been seen elsewhere, the judge turned down every appeal against their conviction and death sentence.

>> practice questions

1   What problems did Prohibition lead to in the 1920s?

2   Why was the Ku Klux Klan able to carry out its violent attacks in the Southern states of the USA during the 1920s?

From boom to bust

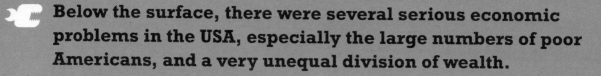

- Below the surface, there were several serious economic problems in the USA, especially the large numbers of poor Americans, and a very unequal division of wealth.

- There were also problems of over-production and speculation.

- When a serious crisis occurred in 1929, Hoover (the Republican President) at first did nothing. Soon, the USA, and the world, was in the grip of a depression.

A The Wall Street Crash

1 **key fact** The US economy had five main weaknesses, despite the 1920s boom.

1 Sixty per cent of US families lived below the poverty line and so could not afford to buy consumer goods – the big trusts kept wages low.

2 The richest people (5 per cent owned 33 per cent of US wealth) **had soon bought all they needed.**

3 US industry found it difficult to export when **other countries put tariffs on US goods in retaliation against US tariffs.**

4 **Competition from Australia and Argentina**, and the **increased use of cars and synthetic fabrics**, led to **reduced sales and over-production of farm products**. Prices fell – many farmers were evicted and many farm workers lost their jobs.

5 Many who lost their jobs had bought consumer goods on **HP**. With no wages (and no unemployment benefits), they were unable to keep up payments and the **goods were repossessed – so increasing the amount of over-production.**

remember >>

Some people (by illegal evasion known as 'skulduggery') bought up sufficient shares to control many industries. So, if they lost money, many different companies would be hit at once.

2 **key fact** This over-production was made more dangerous by a boom in share prices that encouraged millions of people to buy shares.

By 1929, over 20 million people owned shares. Many 'speculators' bought their shares **'on the margin'**, while ordinary people bought them on **HP**.

In the autumn of 1929, some investors (including banks) lost confidence and began panic selling shares – this led to prices tumbling.

This became known as the **Wall Street Crash**. On 24 October ('Black Thursday'), 13 million shares were sold; on 29 October, 16 million were sold.

B Hoover and the Great Depression

① **key fact** As people lost their jobs, a vicious circle began in which sales fell and even more people became unemployed. This led to what became known as the Great Depression.

- By 1933 (the worst year), industrial production had fallen by 40 per cent and unemployment had reached 14 million.

- Many farmers, unable to keep up mortgage payments, were evicted. The situation in the Mid-West was made worse by the **Dust Bowl**.

② **key fact** The Republican President, Herbert Hoover, believed in laissez-faire and rugged individualism – so, at first, he did very little to deal with the problems.

- Without unemployment benefit, many people relied on **soup kitchens** and **charity handouts** and lived in **Hoovervilles** (shanty towns of homes made from cardboard).

- Veteran soldiers tried to persuade Hoover to pay their war pensions early – in 1932, 20 000 veterans (the '**Bonus Army**') marched to Washington and built a Hooverville outside the White House. Hoover ordered the army to break it up.

- Eventually, though, Hoover began to take some action – **in 1930, he cut taxes** and, **in 1931, he gave money to states** to help build dams to provide work. **In 1932, he agreed to an Emergency Relief and Reconstruction Act**, which offered money to states that wished to help the unemployed. But it was too little, too late.

remember >>

The Crash bankrupted many investors. Others lost their savings when smaller banks collapsed. Many companies closed, increasing unemployment.

>> practice questions

Study Source A below, then answer the question that follows.

Year	Unemployed (millions)	Percentage of workforce
1928	2.1	4.4
1930	4.3	9
1931	8.0	16
1932	12.0	24
1933	13	25

Source A: Unemployment figures in the USA, 1928–33, compiled from official government statistics

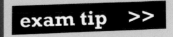
exam tip >>

Make precise references to the information given by the source.

What can you learn from Source A about the effectiveness of Hoover's policies to deal with the Great Depression?

Roosevelt and the New Deal

 The November 1932 presidential elections were won by Franklin Delano Roosevelt, a Democrat. Although he had no specific policies, he promised a 'New Deal'.

Most ordinary people approved of Roosevelt's New Deal laws, but his actions were opposed by some powerful groups.

A New Deal policies

1 **key fact** Unlike Hoover, Roosevelt believed that the government should intervene and spend huge sums of money to end the economic crisis and help the American people.

- However, the US Constitution at that time stated that a newly elected president could not take over for four months – this time was known as the **lame duck months**. During that time, Hoover took limited steps to deal with the Depression.

- By the time Roosevelt took over as President in March 1933, the situation had worsened – unemployment had reached 15 million, and thousands of banks had collapsed.

- Roosevelt summoned Congress to meet in an emergency session during his **First Hundred Days** in order to pass a series of laws to end the crisis.

- His first step was the **Emergency Banking Act**. This closed weaker banks and helped the stronger ones. It was designed to restore confidence in the banking system.

- **The Economy Act** cut the salaries of government employees and set up the **Securities Exchange Commission** to prevent reckless speculation in shares.

> **remember >>**
>
> Roosevelt broadcast 'fireside chats' on the radio to explain his actions to the people.

2 **key fact** Roosevelt then set up a series of government agencies, known as the Alphabet Agencies, to deal with the various problems. These were designed to help the unemployed, revive the economy and create a fairer society.

The main New Deal agencies were as follows:

- Federal Emergency Relief Agency (FERA)

- Civil Works Administration (CWA)

- Tennessee Valley Authority (TVA)

- Civilian Conservation Corps (CCC)

- National Industrial Recovery Act (NIRA) – this included the Public Works Authority (PWA) and the 'Blue Eagle' scheme

- Agricultural Adjustment Act (AAA)

- Home Owners Loan Corporation (HOLC).

B Reactions to the New Deal

1 key fact While most people approved of Roosevelt's New Deal laws, there were those who opposed his actions.

remember >>

In the 1936 presidential elections, Roosevelt won another massive victory, despite those who opposed his policies.

Republicans, who did not agree with governments interfering with people's lives and the economy, or using tax-payers' money to help the poor and unemployed (they believed people should look after themselves)

Opponents of Roosevelt's New Deal

Radicals, such as Huey Long (who started a 'Share Our Wealth' campaign) and Dr Frances Townsend, also opposed the New Deal, as they believed Roosevelt was not doing enough for poor people

Businessmen/industrialists, who objected to government interference, increased taxation to pay for relief programmes and Roosevelt's attempts to strengthen workers' rights

States' rights supporters, who believed that the federal (central) government was wrong to tell states how to help those suffering from the Depression

The Supreme Court (the most serious opponent). Its nine (mostly Republican) judges ruled that several New Deal laws were unconstitutional as they interfered with the rights of individual states. New Deal laws thrown out by the Supreme Court included the NIRA (1935) and the AAA (1936).

C The second New Deal

1 key fact Opposition to the New Deal, especially from the Supreme Court judges, meant that several of Roosevelt's attempts to help people had to end before they had an opportunity to succeed.

So, in 1935, Roosevelt began a second New Deal to extend the first one, and to replace those laws thrown out by the Supreme Court. These new laws included:

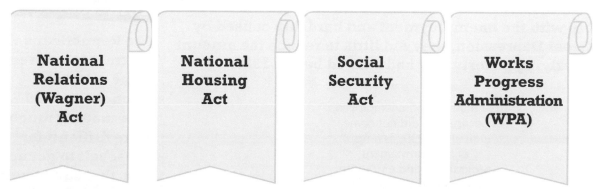

National Relations (Wagner) Act

National Housing Act

Social Security Act

Works Progress Administration (WPA)

>> practice questions

1 Why did many US radicals oppose the New Deal?

2 Why did Roosevelt begin a second New Deal in 1935?

exam tip >>

Remember to give detailed and precise facts to support your explanation.

From Depression to war

- Although the New Deal reduced unemployment from its peak in 1933, problems remained.

- It was really the rearmament programme and entry into the Second World War that finally ended unemployment in the USA.

- US involvement in the Second World War was closely connected to its plans for expansion in Asia, which brought it into competition with Japan.

- Increasing tensions between the USA and Japan culminated in the Japanese attack on the US naval base at Pearl Harbor.

A Success of the New Deal

1 key fact
Despite all the various New Deal laws, by 1937 consumer spending was still only 75 per cent of that in 1929.

- However, because unemployment was falling, Roosevelt's critics tried to get him to **reduce government spending**.

- In 1937, Roosevelt cut back on government-funded projects, because he believed the Depression was ending, and he wanted to **avoid government debt**.

- Unfortunately, this decision coincided with a **further decline in world trade**. As a result, **a second depression began in 1938** and unemployment rose again – by 1939, there were 9.5 million unemployed.

2 key fact
Although the New Deal laws did much to help with the unemployment and hardship caused by the Great Depression, they did little to reduce the amount of underlying poverty that had existed before 1929.

For many of the unemployed, secure jobs did not come until after 1939, as a result of the **rearmament programme and entry into the Second World War**.

Although the destruction of 'surplus' food and animals helped farmers, the **higher prices made food too expensive for many poor people**.

POVERTY

Production quotas set by the AAA **led to millions of poor Black farmers being forced off the land**.

New Deal laws **allowed women and Black Americans to be paid less than white men** – this affected millions of unskilled workers.

> **remember >>**
>
> The Republicans won control of Congress in the mid-term elections in 1938. This made it much more difficult for Roosevelt to get new laws through to help the unemployed during this second depression.

① **key fact** In the 1920s, the Republicans had been supporters of the foreign policy of isolationism.

- However, while Republican presidents had rejected too much involvement with Europe after the war, **this did not apply to other areas of the world**.

- During the 1920s and 1930s, Republican presidents sent the US army into several states in Latin and Central America and the Caribbean (which the US saw as their 'backyard').

- In addition, US plans to expand in **Asia** brought **conflict with Japan**. In particular, the USA objected when Japan invaded Manchuria in 1931.

- Also, despite isolationism, the Republicans had maintained some involvement in Europe – **the Dawes Plan (1924), the Young Plan (1929)** and **the Kellogg–Briand Pact (1928)**.

② **key fact** Roosevelt continued with isolationism at first – in 1934, the Johnson Act forbade loans to countries involved in wars, and two Neutrality Acts were passed in 1935 and 1937.

- However, the USA had its own interests in China, and Roosevelt objected when Japan invaded mainland **China** in 1937.

- **In November 1939**, after the outbreak of war in Europe, Congress agreed to a **Cash and Carry Plan** and, **in 1941, the Lend-Lease Act**, which 'sold' weapons to Britain.

- In Asia, Japanese plans for an economic empire led the USA to impose a **trade boycott on Japan.** In May 1941, the USA imposed an **oil and steel embargo** and **'froze' Japanese assets in the USA.**

- Roosevelt also ordered the strengthening of US military bases in Hawaii and the Philippines.

- Finally, **Japan attacked the US naval base at Pearl Harbor on 7 December 1941**. The USA declared war on Japan on 8 December and, on 11 December, on Germany and Italy.

> **remember >>**
>
> **The US Pacific fleet, with its main base in Pearl Harbor in Hawaii, was the main threat to Japanese ambitions in Asia and the Pacific.**

>> practice questions

Study Source A below, then answer the question that follows.

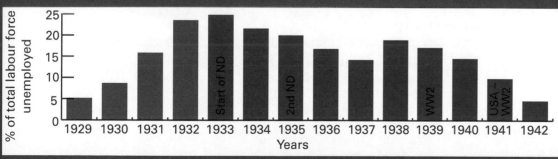

Source A: Unemployment figures for the USA, 1929–42

What can you learn from this graph about the impact of the New Deal on unemployment in the USA?

Causes of the war

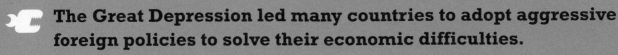

- The Great Depression led many countries to adopt aggressive foreign policies to solve their economic difficulties.

- After Hitler came to power in 1933, his plans to overturn the terms of the Treaty of Versailles led to increased tensions in Europe.

- The failure of the League of Nations to prevent aggression in the early 1930s led Hitler to take increasingly bold actions after 1935.

A Growing tensions, 1930–5

1 key fact The League of Nations became increasingly ineffective during the 1930s as the Depression affected more and more countries.

- The first real example of the League's ineffectiveness was its failure to prevent Japan's invasion and subsequent occupation of **Manchuria in 1931**.

- Tensions in Europe increased **after 1933, when Hitler and the Nazis came to power in Germany.**

- At first, however, Hitler's actions were opposed by a united front that included Britain, France and Italy.

2 key fact Hitler's main aims were to overturn the Treaty of Versailles, unite all German-speakers in a 'Greater Germany' and take 'living space' in Eastern Europe. All these aims would involve war.

One of Hitler's first acts in 1933 was to **take Germany out of the World Disarmament Conference**, which had begun in 1932. Later in 1933, he **took Germany out of the League, and began secret rearmament**.

Once he was securely in power in Germany after June 1934 (Night of the Long Knives), Hitler decided to take more aggressive steps.

However, his **attempt to achieve Anschluss with Austria in 1934** was blocked by France and Britain, and by Italy (which, although a Fascist state, did not want a strong Germany to control Austria).

> **remember >>**
>
> Hitler and the Nazis were violently opposed to Communism – so the main new areas of 'living space' (Lebensraum) were to be taken from the USSR once it had been defeated.

B The Stresa Front

>> **key fact**
Later, in 1934, Britain, France and Italy formed the Stresa Front to oppose any future German aggression.

- This loose alliance broke up in 1935, when Britain and France reluctantly opposed **Italy's invasion of Abyssinia**.

- It was further weakened when Britain signed a **naval treaty** with Nazi Germany later that year. This was partly because the British government disapproved of a military agreement that France had just signed with the USSR.

- Hitler's plans for war were strengthened in **1935** when **the Saarland** voted to return to Germany. The Saarland's iron and coal deposits were essential for German rearmament and industrial recovery. Hitler then began to rearm openly, in defiance of the Treaty of Versailles.

C Hitler's actions, 1936–8

>> **key fact**
Hitler was encouraged in his actions by the League's failure to take effective action against Japanese and Italian aggression, and by the lack of unity between Britain and France. As a result, after 1935, his actions became bolder.

- In **March 1936**, he ordered German troops to **reoccupy the Rhineland** which, since 1919, had been a demilitarised zone. This was a clear violation of the Treaty of Versailles.

- In July 1936, the **Spanish Civil War** began – in August, Hitler and Mussolini decided to intervene on the side of the right-wing Nationalists. Hitler used this war as an opportunity to test German military equipment.

- In **October 1936**, the Stresa Front collapsed completely when cooperation between the two Fascist dictators increased, as **Hitler persuaded Mussolini to sign the Rome–Berlin Axis with Nazi Germany**.

- Then, in **October 1937**, Italy signed the **Anti-Comintern Pact**, which Germany and Japan had already formed in November 1936, promising cooperation in the defence against the USSR – there was now a **Rome–Berlin–Tokyo Axis**.

- With friendship now established between Italy and Germany, Hitler began to cause trouble in Austria by encouraging the Austrian Nazi Party. Finally, in **March 1938**, Hitler made a second attempt at **Anschluss with Austria**. This time, it was successful – again, despite it being against the Treaty of Versailles, Britain and France took no action. Hitler now turned his attention to **Czechoslovakia**.

> **remember >>**
>
> Despite the League having formed a Non-Intervention Committee, Britain and France took no action to prevent Hitler and Mussolini from intervening in the Spanish Civil War.

>> practice questions

1 What important step did Hitler take in March 1936?

2 Which country was taken over by Nazi Germany in March 1938?

Final steps to war

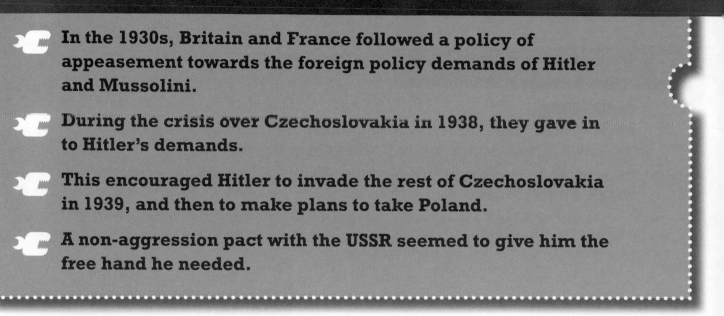

- In the 1930s, Britain and France followed a policy of appeasement towards the foreign policy demands of Hitler and Mussolini.

- During the crisis over Czechoslovakia in 1938, they gave in to Hitler's demands.

- This encouraged Hitler to invade the rest of Czechoslovakia in 1939, and then to make plans to take Poland.

- A non-aggression pact with the USSR seemed to give him the free hand he needed.

A The Czech crisis

1 key fact Appeasement was based on keeping Mussolini and Hitler happy, by agreeing to most of their demands for land and 'revising' the Treaty of Versailles.

- Hitler noticed the **League of Nations' weakness** over Japan's invasion of **Manchuria in 1931**, and Mussolini's invasion of **Abyssinia in 1935**.

- He had also been encouraged by the League's lack of action over his **rearmament** and, in 1936, **his reoccupation of the Rhineland**.

2 key fact In 1938, Hitler began moves against Czechoslovakia. In April, the 'Czech crisis' began when Hitler threatened the Sudetenland, which, since 1919, had been part of Czechoslovakia.

- The Sudetenland had belonged to the Habsburg empire and contained **three million German-speakers**. Hitler encouraged the local Nazis (led by Henlein) to stir up opposition to the Czech government. Hitler then threatened to invade in order to 'protect' these German-speakers.

- France had set up the **Little Entente** with Czechoslovakia and the other Successor States in 1925, promising help if they were threatened by Germany.

- But, in 1938, Daladier (the new French Prime Minister) ignored the agreement – partly because Chamberlain (Prime Minister of Britain) made it clear he would not support any French action.

- Instead, Chamberlain flew to Germany three times in September when Hitler increased his demands. Finally, Britain and France signed the **Munich Agreement**, accepting a German takeover. This gave Hitler the **Czech border defences and armaments works**. The Czechs were not invited to the Munich Conference.

> ### remember >>
>
> Historians are divided over whether appeasement made the Second World War more likely (by encouraging Hitler), or whether Chamberlain acted wisely in view of Britain's inability to fight a war in 1938.

B Crisis over Poland

① key fact After the Munich Agreement, Hitler threatened the rest of Czechoslovakia. In March 1939, German troops invaded.

- Once again, Britain and France took no action. Hitler concluded that, provided he accepted Germany's western borders, he was free to expand eastwards.

- Hitler's next target was **Poland**, but, at the end of March, Britain and France promised to defend Polish independence. Hitler did not take this seriously, even when Britain introduced conscription for all males aged 20–21.

② key fact Hitler then worked to get an agreement with the USSR in order to prevent it opposing his plans to invade Poland. He believed that, without Soviet help, Britain and France would not assist Poland.

Since 1935, Stalin had been trying to get an agreement with Britain and France. Even after the Munich Agreement, he had tried to secure an agreement to stop Hitler's growing demands.

However, he became increasingly suspicious when Britain delayed further discussions in the summer of 1939. He wondered if Britain and France were prepared to accept German conquests in the East – and even suspected that they were secretly encouraging Hitler to attack the USSR.

This pact included **a secret clause to divide Poland between Germany and the USSR**, and to allow the USSR to take over **the Baltic states**. This extra territory was to give the USSR a **buffer zone** against the expected German invasion.

So, in August 1939, in order to obtain more time to build up Soviet defences, Stalin agreed to a **ten-year non-aggression pact** with Nazi Germany (also known as the **Nazi–Soviet**, or the **Molotov–Ribbentrop Pact**, after the Soviet and German foreign ministers who signed the agreement).

> **remember >>**
>
> In the early stages of the Czech crisis, Stalin had promised help, if Britain and France agreed to take action over the Sudetenland. But he was not even invited to the Munich Conference.

>> practice questions

Study Source A, then answer the questions that follow.

The international conference at Munich in 1938 had a practical task: to solve the problem of the three million German-speakers in Czechoslovakia and so prevent a European war. The Munich Agreement signed at the Conference succeeded in this task. The Czechoslovak territory inhabited by the three million Germans was transferred to Germany. The Germans were satisfied, there was no war.

Source A: Extract from *The Myths of Munich*, published by British historian A.J.P. Taylor in 1969

1 Briefly explain the reference to 'three million German-speakers'.

2 Briefly explain the reference to the 'Munich Agreement'.

Early stages

 The Second World War began in September 1939, when Germany invaded Poland.

 Nazi Germany had early successes using 'Blitzkrieg' methods.

 By 1940, Britain was on its own; then, in 1941, Hitler attacked the USSR.

A   The war in Europe

1 **key fact** On 1 September 1939, German troops invaded Poland. Two days later, Britain and France declared war on Germany – the Second World War had begun. Poland was defeated in less than a month.

surprise

planes

tanks

speed

German 'Blitzkrieg' ('lightning war') tactics quickly knocked out an enemy

overwhelming force

paratroops   motorised infantry

2 **key fact** However, despite Britain and France's agreement with Poland, they did not send help and, until April 1940, were not really involved in the war. This period is therefore sometimes known as the 'Phoney War'.

In April, **Denmark was occupied and Norway invaded by Germany** – a small British force failed to prevent German control of the region. In May, Norway surrendered and Hitler ordered invasions of the Low Countries and France.

By the end of May, the **Netherlands, Belgium and Luxembourg** had been defeated, and the British Expeditionary Force (sent to help France) had to be evacuated from Dunkirk in **Operation Dynamo**.

remember >>

Britain and France took no action against Nazi Germany during the Phoney War, even though German U-boats and mines sunk several Allied ships.

Britain was now on its own. Despite winning the Battle of Britain, it remained without allies until June 1941.

On 22 June, **France surrendered**. The Germans occupied northern France, while Marshal Petain was allowed to run the south (called 'Vichy France'), provided he cooperated with the Germans.

Hitler's early successes encouraged **Mussolini to declare war on Britain and France**.

B The Eastern Front

① key fact On 22 June 1941, Hitler launched his long-term plan (Operation Barbarossa) to invade the USSR.

- The USSR was taken by surprise, as Stalin believed Hitler would not attack until Britain had been defeated. As a result, the Germans – with an army over five million strong – destroyed most of the Soviet airforce on the ground, and advanced deep into the Soviet Union. Over 700 000 Red Army troops were captured.

- However, this attack turned the USSR into an ally for Britain, so ending Britain's isolation.

- By October 1941, the USSR seemed about to collapse. However, as the Russians retreated, they moved factories and workers behind the Ural Mountains. What they couldn't remove, they destroyed (**scorched earth policy**).

② key fact An important turning point came when the Russian winter began early – the German army, not equipped for a winter campaign, ground to a halt. The Red Army then launched a counter-attack in December 1941.

- Hitler ordered new offensives and devoted over 75 per cent of his forces to the Eastern Front. In June 1942, he split his southern army into two, as he was determined to capture Stalingrad.

- From November 1942 to January 1943, the Russians fought back. Finally, what remained of the German Sixth Army at Stalingrad was forced to surrender.

- The **Battle of Stalingrad** was an important turning point in the war. In July, the Russians won the **Battle of Kursk** (the biggest tank battle in history) and, from September 1943, the Germans were in retreat. Over 90 per cent of Germany's total military casualties were on the Eastern Front.

>> practice questions

Study the map, then answer the questions that follow.

1 Explain why Operation Barbarossa had not been successful by December 1941.

2 Explain why the Battle of Stalingrad in the winter of 1942–3 was important.

exam tip >>

Don't just describe what happened – you must give reasons why something was (or was not) successful or important.

AG = Army group   N = North

C = Central   S = South

The tide begins to turn

 In the early 1940s, the crucial naval Battle of the Atlantic took place. This was Germany's attempt to prevent US military supplies reaching Britain.

But, by 1943, this had been won effectively by the Allies.

By then, the Allies had also taken control of North Africa, and were preparing to invade Italy.

A Battle of the Atlantic

1 key fact Before becoming involved directly in the war in December 1941, the USA ended its policy of isolationism and neutrality when, in March 1941, Roosevelt decided to loan military equipment to Britain via the Lend-Lease Scheme.

At first, this equipment had to be carried in British ships. But **after Pearl Harbor**, US ships also transported supplies to Britain.	It was therefore important for Nazi Germany to prevent these vital supplies reaching Britain from the USA. This naval contest became known as the **Battle of the Atlantic**.	At first, German U-boats succeeded in destroying large numbers of these merchant ships. This was despite Allied tactics, which involved using a convoy system and faster convoy ships, with destroyers providing protection for merchant ships.	These heavy losses led to severe shortages of food and raw materials in Britain. By March 1943, it seemed as if Britain was losing the ability to continue with the war.

2 key fact However, an important turning point took place in April 1943, when German radio codes were broken by the Allies.

- From May, the Allies began to destroy almost fifty German submarines a month. This success was also the result of using better tactics and technology, such as:
  - faster escort ships
  - radar and asdic to find submarines
  - long-range aircraft.
- In March 1944, the Germans ended their attacks on convoys – the **Battle of the Atlantic had been won by the Allies.**

B North Africa and Italy

① key fact In August 1940, an Italian army occupied British Somaliland and, in September, a 240 000-strong army invaded Egypt in order to capture the Suez Canal. This began an important military contest, as the canal was a vital British shipping route, especially for oil.

- In October, Italy invaded Greece. But the Italians did badly and had to divert troops from Africa. In December 1940, a British counter-attack in Egypt resulted in the capture of the Italian colony of Libya.

- In the Balkans, Yugoslavia (unlike Romania, Hungary and Bulgaria) refused to ally with Hitler. In April 1941, Germany invaded Yugoslavia, and Greece, in order to help the Italians. By the end of May, both Yugoslavia and Greece had been defeated.

② key fact The importance of North Africa was shown in April 1941, when Hitler sent the Afrika Korps, commanded by Rommel, to Africa to help the Italians. Soon, Libya had been retaken, and Rommel invaded Egypt.

- In June 1941, with most of Germany's military resources on the Eastern Front, the British launched an unsuccessful offensive against the Afrika Korps.

- However, **Operation Crusader**, launched by Britain in November 1941, was successful at first and ended the siege of Tobruk. But, in May 1942, Rommel defeated the British Eighth Army at Tobruk.

- In August, Montgomery took charge of the Eighth Army, and, in October/November 1942, defeated Rommel at the **Battle of El Alamein**.

- This proved a turning point, and the Afrika Korps began to retreat. The Allies then launched **Operation Torch** – Rommel surrendered in Tunisia and, by May 1943, the Allies controlled North Africa. From 1943, Axis forces were also being slowly pushed out of the Balkans.

- This allowed an Anglo-American **invasion of Sicily** in July. In September, the **invasion of mainland Italy** began. Mussolini was overthrown and Italy sided with the Allies. But Hitler sent German forces to slow the Allies – this German army mounted a determined resistance in Italy until May 1945.

remember >>

At the same time that the Allies were taking control of North Africa in 1943, Axis forces were also retreating from the Balkans.

>> practice questions

1 Why were Rommel's Afrika Korps reinforcements sent to North Africa in 1941?

2 What military campaign followed the success of Operation Torch in North Africa?

The closing stages

Two other decisive turning points took place in 1942 and 1943 – the end of Japanese expansion in Asia and the increased bombing of Germany.

These allowed further Allied advances in 1944–5, which finally ended the war.

A War in Asia and the Pacific

1 key fact In December 1941, Japan had launched a surprise attack on the main base of the US Pacific Fleet at Pearl Harbor, bringing the USA into the war.

- Since 1931, Japan (with the third largest army in the world) had been expanding in Asia. The USA, which had long had its own interests in the region, objected to **Japan's invasion of China in 1937**.

- The invasion of China was expensive, so Japan decided to take over parts of South-East Asia to form a **Greater East Asia Co-prosperity Sphere**, which would provide Japan with oil and other raw materials.

2 key fact When Japan invaded French Indo-China in July 1941, the USA banned the sale of oil, aircraft and iron to Japan, and froze all Japanese assets in the USA until Japan made peace with China.

- **Oil and iron existed in the British and Dutch colonies** in the region, but Japan's navy was not strong enough to face a combined Anglo-American force.

- The Japanese attack on Pearl Harbor had been intended to deliver such a blow to the US Pacific fleet that it could not stop Japan's takeover of those British and Dutch colonies.

- At first, Japanese forces were victorious in South-East Asia and, by August 1942, had conquered most of the region.

> **remember >>**
>
> The Japanese attack on Pearl Harbor turned the Pacific War into part of the Second World War.

3 key fact However, in May 1942, Japan suffered its first defeat at the Battle of Midway. This ended Japanese naval supremacy and allowed US forces to advance.

- In June 1943, the USA began submarine warfare against Japanese shipping.

- From January 1944, Allied forces used the tactic of **island hopping** – ignoring the smaller islands occupied by Japan in order to concentrate forces on the more strategically important ones.

B D-Day and A-bombs

① key fact There were Allied offensives in both Europe and Asia in 1943.

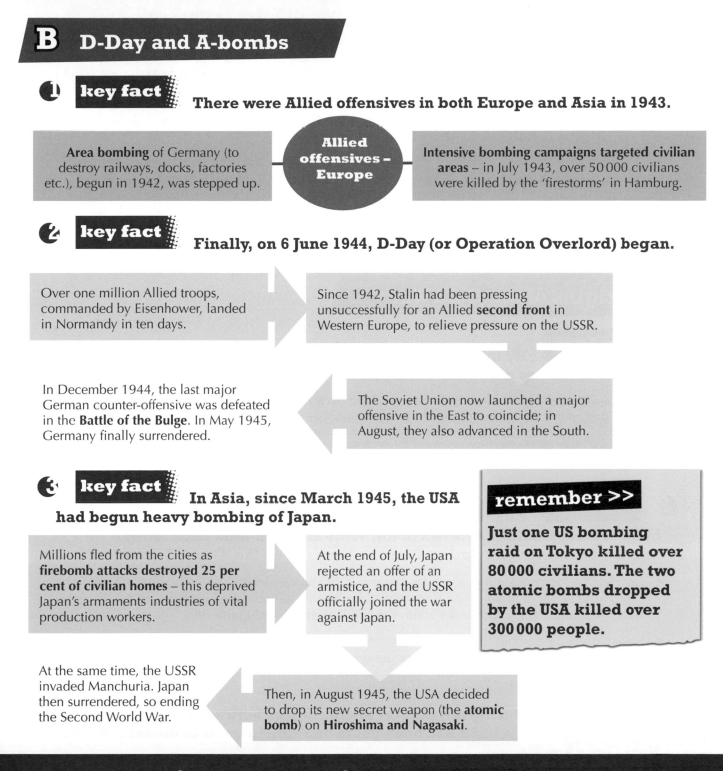

Area bombing of Germany (to destroy railways, docks, factories etc.), begun in 1942, was stepped up.

Allied offensives – Europe

Intensive bombing campaigns targeted civilian **areas** – in July 1943, over 50 000 civilians were killed by the 'firestorms' in Hamburg.

② key fact Finally, on 6 June 1944, D-Day (or Operation Overlord) began.

Over one million Allied troops, commanded by Eisenhower, landed in Normandy in ten days.

Since 1942, Stalin had been pressing unsuccessfully for an Allied **second front** in Western Europe, to relieve pressure on the USSR.

In December 1944, the last major German counter-offensive was defeated in the **Battle of the Bulge**. In May 1945, Germany finally surrendered.

The Soviet Union now launched a major offensive in the East to coincide; in August, they also advanced in the South.

③ key fact In Asia, since March 1945, the USA had begun heavy bombing of Japan.

Millions fled from the cities as **firebomb attacks destroyed 25 per cent of civilian homes** – this deprived Japan's armaments industries of vital production workers.

At the end of July, Japan rejected an offer of an armistice, and the USSR officially joined the war against Japan.

At the same time, the USSR invaded Manchuria. Japan then surrendered, so ending the Second World War.

Then, in August 1945, the USA decided to drop its new secret weapon (the **atomic bomb**) on **Hiroshima and Nagasaki**.

remember >>

Just one US bombing raid on Tokyo killed over 80 000 civilians. The two atomic bombs dropped by the USA killed over 300 000 people.

>> practice questions

Study Source A below, then answer the question that follows.

The use of this barbarous weapon at Hiroshima and Nagasaki was of no material assistance … the Japanese were already defeated … because of … the successful bombing with conventional weapons.

Source A: Extract from the memoirs of Admiral Leahy, US Chief of Staff in 1945

What does this source tell us about the attitudes of the US military in 1945 to the dropping of atomic bombs in August 1945?

The early stages of the Cold War

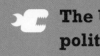 The USA and the USSR believed in two different economic and political systems – capitalism and communism.

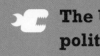 Although such differences had been pushed into the background during the Second World War, mutual suspicions began to re-emerge even before the defeat of Germany and Japan.

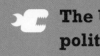 Some agreements were made at important conferences, but later conferences saw big differences in post-war aims between the USSR and the other members of the Grand Alliance.

A Origins of the Cold War

1 **key fact** By the end of the Second World War, the USA and the USSR were the two dominant superpowers.

- European countries that had been powerful before the war, such as Britain, France and Germany, were now economically weakened or in ruins.

- However, the two superpowers were by no means equal in strength, as the **USA had avoided the destruction suffered by the USSR.**

2 **key fact** Although the USA and the USSR were allies, there had been several tensions between them, some of which went back to 1917 and the Bolshevik Revolution. This has been called the 'Great Contest'.

- Capitalist countries, such as the USA, believe in private ownership of the economy and (normally) political democracy. Communists believe in state ownership of the main industried and banks, and under Stalin the USSR operated one-party rule.

- Soviet suspicions about the West had increased after 1933, as Stalin had felt that **Britain and France, by appeasement, were encouraging Hitler to attack the USSR.**

3 **key fact** During the war, these differences between the USA, Britain and the USSR had been put to one side in order to defeat Nazi Germany.

- However, disagreements over the opening of a **second front** emerged in the Grand Alliance after 1942.

- Stalin became increasingly suspicious about the **delay in opening up** this second front against Nazi Germany in Western Europe.

- Stalin was desperate for this, to relieve pressure on the USSR. By 1944, there were 228 Axis divisions on the Eastern Front, compared to 61 in Western Europe.

④ **key fact** Immediately after the end of the war, both sides began to distrust each other's motives.

- With the Soviet economy in ruins and over 25 million people dead, Stalin feared the **USA might use its monopoly of nuclear weapons** to destroy the USSR, which was the only Communist state in the world.

- On the other hand, the USA and the West feared that **Stalin would try to spread Communism** across war-devastated Europe and so destroy capitalism and opportunities for investments and profits.

remember >>

Since 1914, the Soviet Union had been invaded three times through Eastern Europe.

B Conferences, 1943–5

>> **key fact** Three major conferences between the Allies took place in the period 1943–5.

remember >>

When Roosevelt died in April 1945, he was replaced by Vice-President Truman, who took a more anti-Communist line.

Tehran Conference, November 1943

Despite the continued delay in opening a second front, the 'Big Three' reached outline agreements on redrawing the Polish borders, and on preventing any anti-Soviet alliance in Eastern Europe after the war.

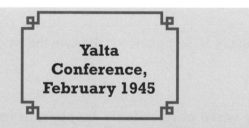

Yalta Conference, February 1945

Initial agreements over Poland and Germany (including reparations) were reached. Stalin also agreed to join the war against Japan once Germany had been defeated.

Potsdam Conference, July–August 1945

Germany had now been defeated. This time, serious differences emerged over German reparations, the government of Poland and the presence of the Red Army in Eastern Europe. However, there was an agreement that the USSR could receive eastern Poland, while Poland would be compensated with German territory.

>> practice questions

Why was Stalin less pleased with the outcome of the Potsdam Conference than with the agreements reached previously at Tehran and Yalta?

The Cold War begins

- Within a year of the war ending, growing tensions between the Allies resulted in the start of what became known as the Cold War.

- While the USSR began to take control of Eastern Europe, the USA adopted a policy of 'containment' of Communism – in Europe and the rest of the world.

- The Cold War soon led to an arms race, and even to 'hot' wars in various parts of the world.

A Early tensions

① key fact During the Potsdam Conference, Truman decided to drop atomic bombs on Japan without informing Stalin.

- Truman also decided not to share the technology of this secret weapon with the USSR. Although Stalin ordered Soviet scientists to build a Soviet bomb, the **USA had a nuclear monopoly for the next four years**.

- Stalin feared the USA would use its superiority to **blackmail the war-devastated Soviet Union**.

② key fact One Soviet response was to step up its control of Eastern Europe. This took place between 1945 and 1948.

- Stalin said these moves were to create **buffer zones** to give the USSR greater protection from any future invasion.

- The West, however, saw these moves as the first stage in Stalin's plans to take over the whole of Europe.

③ key fact Differences over Germany were particularly important in the breakdown of relations between the USSR and the West.

remember >>

In 1944, Churchill made the 'percentages agreement' on spheres of influence with Stalin – this accepted Soviet influence in most of Eastern Europe.

- The USSR wanted substantial reparations and was reluctant to allow Germany to re-industrialise. But **the USA now opposed massive reparations**, and instead wanted to rebuild the German economy as quickly as possible.

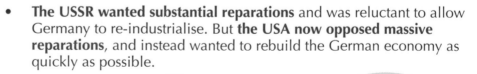

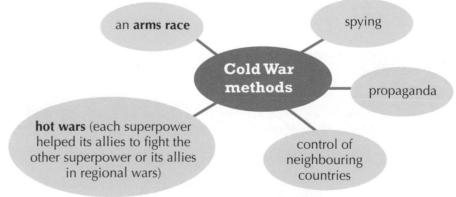

an **arms race**   spying   **Cold War methods**   propaganda   **hot wars** (each superpower helped its allies to fight the other superpower or its allies in regional wars)   control of neighbouring countries

B The origins of 'containment'

① key fact During 1946, Truman decided to adopt the new policy of 'containment' of Communism.

- In **February 1946, Kennan**, a US diplomat, had sent a report to the US government about the USSR. This **Long Telegram** said that the Soviet Union was determined to expand.

- Politicians and advisers who believed (as Roosevelt had) that Stalin was prepared to make concessions in return for security were forced to resign.

② key fact By 1947, most West European countries were in a serious economic crisis, and Communist parties in Italy and France were winning votes in elections.

- Then, in February 1947, Britain said it could no longer afford to support the Greek Royalists in their civil war against the Greek Communists.

- The USA, believing in the **rotten apple** theory (similar to the 'domino theory'), feared that if Greece went Communist, other countries would follow.

C The Truman Doctrine and the Marshall Plan

>> key fact In 1947, Truman announced two policies that were intended to 'contain' the spread of Communism.

- **The Truman Doctrine**, in March, said that the USA would give military help to all countries resisting 'armed minorities' or 'outside pressure'.

- **The Marshall Plan, or Marshall Aid**, was announced in June 1947 in order to give massive economic aid to Western Europe. This had four main aims:

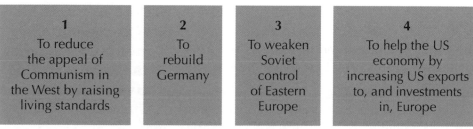

1	2	3	4
To reduce the appeal of Communism in the West by raising living standards	To rebuild Germany	To weaken Soviet control of Eastern Europe	To help the US economy by increasing US exports to, and investments in, Europe

remember >>

As part of the new policy of 'containment', Truman also set up the National Security Council (NSC) and the Central Intelligence Agency (CIA).

- Although aid was available to all countries, the conditions for receiving aid (such as US supervision and companies to be privately owned) meant the USSR did not, in the end, take part in the scheme.

>> practice questions

1 List the four main aims of the Marshall Plan.

2 Why did the USSR not benefit from Marshall Aid?

Increasing tensions, 1946–9

- As Cold War tensions developed after 1945, Stalin decided to increase Soviet control of Eastern Europe.

- At the same time, a serious crisis broke out over Germany, and especially Berlin.

- This crisis then led to the division of Germany, the formation of alliances and a new arms race.

A The 'Iron Curtain' and the Berlin Blockade

① key fact After 1945, Stalin felt particularly vulnerable as the Soviet Union had suffered great destruction during the war, whereas the USA was the world's richest power.

- Using rigged elections and other methods, Stalin ensured that Communists came to power in Eastern European countries and would accept Soviet control. This would give the USSR a **buffer zone** in any future war.

- In 1946, Bulgaria was the first to have a Communist-dominated government. In 1947, Hungary, Poland and Romania followed. The last Eastern European country to come under Communist control was Czechoslovakia, in 1948.

② key fact Stalin also feared the USA's desire to revive Germany, which, since 1900, had twice invaded the USSR.

- Although Germany had temporarily been split into four administrative zones, it had been agreed at Potsdam to treat it as one economic unit.

- However, the question of **reparations** caused growing conflict between the USSR (which wanted massive compensation) and the other Allies (who were against this).

- **In January 1947, the USA and Britain merged their zones to form Bizonia** – Stalin feared this was the first step to reviving the economy of a new West German state.

- As Bizonia contained 75 per cent of Germany's population and most of its industry, Stalin saw it as a military threat. These fears increased when France added its zone, to make **Trizonia**.

- Then, **in June 1947, without consulting the USSR, the West introduced a new currency (the Deutsch Mark) into its zones, including West Berlin** (inside the Soviet zone).

> **remember >>**
>
> The division of Germany into West and East soon came to symbolise the Cold War division of Europe into two mutually suspicious and hostile camps divided by the 'Iron Curtain'.

③ key fact This Berlin Crisis was the first serious Cold War conflict between the two sides.

- Stalin was opposed to a separate West German state, and so cut off all transport links to West Berlin. This became known as the **Berlin Blockade**.

- The West responded with the massive **Berlin Airlift**, in which tons of food, fuel and other vital supplies were flown into West Berlin. In May 1949, Stalin called off the blockade.

- This Berlin Crisis speeded up Western moves to set up a separate West German state, and, in **May 1949, the new Federal Republic of Germany** was set up. **In October**, the USSR transformed its eastern zone into the new **German Democratic Republic**.

B Alliances and the arms race

1 key fact In January 1949, towards the end of the Berlin Crisis, the USA became head of the North Atlantic Treaty Organisation (NATO).

- This grew out of the **Brussels Treaty Organisation**, which the countries of Western Europe had formed in **February 1948**, at the height of the Berlin Crisis.

- The USA said NATO was a defensive alliance against the Soviet 'threat'.

2 key fact However, at this time, the USSR was only a regional power, while the USA was already a global power. The USSR's allies were the poor and weak East European states and it had no allies outside Europe.

USSR	USA
The USSR was alarmed by the formation of NATO, especially as the **USA's nuclear monopoly** meant NATO could launch atomic weapons against the USSR.	The formation of NATO intensified the **arms race** (conventional and nuclear) between the two sides.
In 1945, the USSR's Red Army had numbered 11 million. After the war, the Red Army dropped to 3 million, but remained the largest army in Europe.	In 1945, the USA had 12 million troops. After the war, the USA greatly reduced its army, although its forces remained technically superior.
The USSR did not test its first atomic (A) bomb until August 1949.	By August 1949, the USA was already working on a more powerful nuclear weapon – **the hydrogen (H) bomb**.

remember >>

Although NATO was formed in 1949, the USSR had no similar alliance until 1955, when the Warsaw Pact was established. Even after 1955, NATO continued to have overall military superiority.

>> practice questions

1   Why did the Soviet Union insist on massive reparations from Germany at the end of the war?

2   What were the main results of the Berlin Crisis of 1947–9?

Hot spots (1)

- Cold War tensions increased in 1949, when the Chinese Communist Party came to power in China.

- In 1950, the first 'hot war' broke out in Korea. Although both the USA and the USSR were involved on the two opposing sides, there was no direct conflict between them.

- When Stalin died in 1953, there was a slight improvement in relations between East and West, although problems still existed.

A The Korean War

1 key fact After the Communist victory in China, Truman ordered a review of US policy. In April 1950, the NSC 68 document advised Truman to move from 'containment' to the 'roll back' of Communism.

- Tensions were increasing in **Korea**, which, after the war, had been **divided (along the 38th parallel)** into a Communist North and a capitalist South. Both sides were preparing to invade the other to reunify their country.

- Then, in June, North Korea invaded the South and quickly conquered most of it.

2 key fact The USA, believing in the 'domino theory', decided to use the UN to 'contain' this Communist threat.

- The USSR (boycotting the UN in protest at the USA's refusal to allow Communist China a seat) **was unable to veto this**.

- Most of the UN troops were Americans, and the US/UN force was commanded by **US General MacArthur**. By October 1950, North Korean troops had been pushed back over the border.

3 key fact Then, in breach of the UN resolution, Truman ordered MacArthur to invade the North – this was part of the new US policy of 'roll back'.

> **remember >>**
> The Communist victory in China led to US anti-Communist hysteria (McCarthyism).

| When US troops reached the border with China, **the Chinese government sent in an army to help the North.** By January 1951, US/UN forces had been pushed back across the 38th parallel. | A **stalemate** developed. In July 1952, talks for a truce began. Meanwhile, **the USA developed the H-bomb in 1952**. | **In January 1953, Eisenhower became US President**, and in March, **Stalin died.** | **In July 1953, an armistice was finally signed.** Later that month, **the USSR exploded its first H-bomb.** |

B Hungary and the Berlin Wall

① key fact When Stalin died in 1953, the new Soviet leaders had wanted to reduce Cold War tensions, and soon a 'thaw' began. At the same time, Eisenhower became concerned at the risk of nuclear war.

- **In 1955, Khrushchev became overall leader of the USSR.** He believed the Cold War's arms race was too expensive – his policy of **peaceful coexistence** aimed to concentrate on economic competition with the West.

- Khrushchev tried to reduce tensions by agreeing to **end the division of Austria** in return for it not joining NATO.

- But the arms race continued. **So, in 1955, he formed the Warsaw Pact** to counter NATO, which had been set up in 1949.

② key fact In 1956, Khrushchev attacked Stalin's actions at the Twentieth Congress of the Soviet Communist Party. 'De-Stalinisation' then followed in the USSR, and Cominform was ended.

- These moves encouraged Eastern Europeans to think they could reduce Soviet domination. **Some reforms were allowed in Poland.**

- In **Hungary**, huge demonstrations forced Rakosi, a hardliner, to resign. He was replaced by **Nagy**.

- However, when Nagy tried to take Hungary out of the Warsaw Pact, **Soviet forces invaded in November 1956**.

- This **Hungarian Revolt** was crushed. Nagy was deposed and later executed.

- The 'thaw' was further weakened by a **new crisis over Germany and Berlin**, which broke out **in 1958**.

- Relations improved at the **Camp David summit in 1959**, but deteriorated in 1960 because of the **U2 incident**. Thousands of East Germans fled to the West. In 1961, East Germany built the **Berlin Wall** between East and West Berlin.

>> practice questions

Study Sources A and B below, then answer the question that follows.

KOREA, 1950
CHINA, 1949
EAST GERMANY, 1949
CZECHOSLOVAKIA, 1948
HUNGARY, 1947
ROMANIA, 1947
BULGARIA, 1946
POLAND, 1945

Source A: An illustration of the domino theory

Source B: Extract from a speech by US President Truman in 1950, after the invasion of South Korea by North Korea

> The attack on Korea makes it plain beyond all doubt that Communism has passed beyond the use of subversion to conquer independent nations and will now use armed invasion and war.

How useful are Sources A and B as historical evidence of US motives and policies in the Korean War?

Hot spots (2)

- In 1962, a serious crisis broke out over Cuba.

- At the same time, a 'hot war' developed in Vietnam.

- But US attempts to 'contain' Communism in South-East Asia proved to be a costly failure.

A   Cuba and the missile crisis

1   **key fact**   The USA saw Latin America and the Caribbean as its 'backyard'. In 1948, it had set up the Organisation of American States (OAS) to prevent the spread of Communism in the region.

| But, in **Cuba** in **1959**, **Castro** led a victorious revolution against Batista (a corrupt and brutal dictator, supported by the USA). | → | The USA opposed Castro's policies of **land reform** and Cuban **neutrality in the Cold War**. So Eisenhower stopped buying Cuban sugar. **Castro then sold the sugar to the USSR.** |

2   **key fact**   In 1961, the USA helped Cuban exiles in an unsuccessful attempt to invade Cuba. This 'Bay of Pigs' incident led Castro to ask for Soviet protection.

| **Khrushchev**, worried by **US missiles in Turkey**, decided to put Soviet missiles on Cuba (90 miles away from the USA). | → | US spy-planes noticed missile sites (without missiles) in September 1962. **Kennedy** imposed a **naval blockade** to prevent Soviet ships bringing in the missiles. | → | A Third World War seemed near, but the **Cuban Missile Crisis** ended when Khrushchev agreed to withdraw the missiles. |

- In **1963**, a **hot line** between the White House and the Kremlin was set up. **A Nuclear Test Ban Treaty** was also signed.

remember >>

The USSR publicly backed down, but the USA secretly promised not to invade Cuba and to remove its missiles from Turkey.

B The Vietnam War

① key fact Another serious Cold War hot spot was Vietnam, part of the French colony of Indo-China.

- Before 1945, the **Vietminh** (a nationalist army led by the Communist **Ho Chi Minh**) had been fighting for independence. After 1945, because of the Cold War, the USA supported the French.

- In **1954**, the French were defeated at **Dien Bien Phu** and withdrew.

- At the **Geneva Conference**, Vietnam was **temporarily divided along the 17th parallel**, with elections to take place in 1956.

remember >>
The North was ruled by Communists and the South by a landlord class.

② key fact Diem, who became the leader of the South in 1955, refused to hold the elections. In 1960, Communists in the South then formed the Viet Cong to fight Diem.

- The Viet Cong (and North Vietnamese troops) had years of **guerilla warfare** experience against the French and then the Japanese, while the US troops were inexperienced.

- By 1962, Kennedy had greatly increased US aid, but Diem continued to lose ground to the Viet Cong. In November 1963, the CIA encouraged generals in the South to overthrow and murder Diem.

remember >>
North Vietnam and the USSR sent supplies to the South along the Ho Chi Minh Trail.

③ key fact When President Kennedy was assassinated that same month, Vice-President Johnson took over – he was committed to increasing (escalating) US involvement in Vietnam.

- After the **Gulf of Tonkin incident**, the US Congress passed the Tonkin Resolution, allowing Johnson to take 'all necessary steps' to defend South Vietnam.

- In **1965**, Johnson launched massive bombing of North Vietnam (**Operation Rolling Thunder**). By 1969, there were over **500 000 US troops** in South Vietnam. However, in **1968**, the Viet Cong launched the **Tet Offensive**.

④ key fact By then, many people in the USA were opposed to the war and Johnson did not stand in the 1968 elections.

- The new US President, **Nixon**, decided to end US involvement, and began a policy of **Vietnamisation**. However, US bombing raids were stepped up.

- When Cold War relations began to improve in what was called **détente**, peace negotiations began. In 1973, US forces withdrew from Vietnam and, in 1975, Vietnam was finally reunited after the North invaded the South.

>> practice questions

1 What was the significance of the Tet Offensive in 1968?

2 What factors led to the USA's forced withdrawal from Vietnam?

Fluctuations

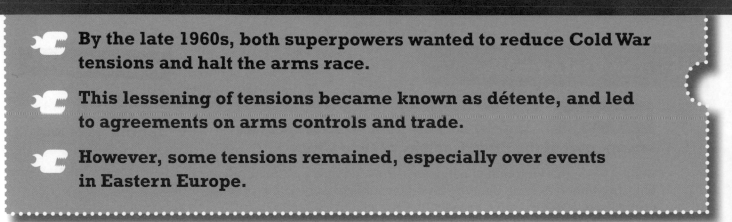

- By the late 1960s, both superpowers wanted to reduce Cold War tensions and halt the arms race.
- This lessening of tensions became known as détente, and led to agreements on arms controls and trade.
- However, some tensions remained, especially over events in Eastern Europe.

A Reasons for détente

Détente developed for five main reasons:

1 The Cuban Missile Crisis, and various weapons systems errors, had brought nuclear war near.

2 There was increased opposition to nuclear weapons, and other countries were developing nuclear weapons.

3 The Soviet economy (less wealthy than the USA's) was struggling under the huge cost of matching the USA's lead in nuclear weapons. The USSR was also worried at signs of growing cooperation between the USA and China.

4 The USA was keen to use China to put pressure on the USSR to make concessions, while China wanted to increase trade with the West, and saw the USA as an ally against the USSR.

5 The USA was also keen to negotiate its withdrawal from Vietnam and to reconsider its Cold War strategy.

remember >>

Despite détente, the arms race continued. There were verification problems with SALT 1, and the USSR often ignored human rights agreed at Helsinki. Despite this, a draft SALT 2 Treaty was agreed in 1978.

B Détente in practice

>> **key fact** Détente was associated with presidents Nixon and Carter in the USA, Brezhnev in the USSR and Mao Zedong in China, and resulted in various agreements in the late 1960s and the 1970s.

The USA allowed Communist China to join the UN, 1971

Nuclear Non-Proliferation Treaty, 1968

Détente agreements

SALT 1 Treaty, 1972, between the USA and the USSR, limited the production of some strategic nuclear weapons

Helsinki Agreement, 1975, confirmed Europe's 1945 borders, and dealt with human rights

C Problems in Eastern Europe

>> key fact Despite détente, Soviet leaders maintained control over Eastern Europe, as events in Czechoslovakia (1968) and in Poland (1980) showed.

Czechoslovakia

- In 1946, the Czech Communist Party won 38 per cent of the vote in free elections. But after 1948, Czechoslovakia was tightly ruled; by the mid-1960s, its economy was stagnating.
- In 1966, Czech students demonstrated for greater political freedom and less Soviet control. In **1968**, reform Communists forced Novotny, a hard-line Stalinist, to resign. He was replaced by **Alexander Dubček**.
- Dubček then announced his **Action Plan** to create **Socialism with a human face**. Controls on the mass media were lifted, and people were allowed to criticise the government.
- This **Prague Spring** led the USSR and some other Eastern European countries to send the **Warsaw Letter,** expressing their fears. Dubček made it clear he would not take Czechoslovakia out of the Warsaw Pact, but he insisted on reform.
- So, in August 1968, Warsaw Pact forces invaded, and Dubček was dismissed. In November, the **Brezhnev Doctrine** said no Warsaw Pact member could leave it and prohibited multiparty systems.

Poland

- In Poland, economic problems in the 1970s led to strikes. In 1980, the government raised food prices.
- Many strikers formed **Solidarity**, an independent trade union. One of its main leaders was **Lech Walesa**. Solidarity began to make political demands that went against the Brezhnev Doctrine.
- This worried the USSR which, in **1981**, put pressure on the Polish Communists to take action. **Martial law was imposed**, Solidarity was banned, and Walesa was arrested.

> **remember >>**
>
> Events in Czechoslovakia did little to undermine détente, but, by 1980, developments elsewhere led to Poland becoming a cause of friction between the Western and Eastern blocs.

>> practice questions

Study Source A, then answer the question that follows.

Source A:
Map showing Czechoslovakia and its neighbours

>
>
> **exam tip >>**
>
> Identify more than one possible reason or factor.

Using the source, and your own knowledge, explain why Warsaw troops marched into Czechoslovakia in 1968.

The end of the Cold War

- By 1979, détente was under increasing strain for a number of reasons.

- In 1980, when Reagan took over from Carter, détente ended as a second Cold War began.

- However, in 1985, Gorbachev became leader of the USSR. He made important concessions on nuclear weapons – these, and the collapse of the USSR in 1991, finally brought an end to the Cold War.

A The second Cold War

key fact An important reason for the end of détente was a series of revolutions in Western Europe (Portugal and Spain) and the developing world (Iran and Nicaragua) during the late 1970s.

- These revolutions deprived the USA of several allies. Although the USSR had not been involved, US politicians blamed the USSR.

- The USA also attacked the USSR for not implementing the Helsinki Agreement on Human Rights.

- Then, **in December 1979, the USSR sent troops into Afghanistan**, to help the new Communist government in its fight against Islamic fundamentalists.

- This was strongly condemned by the US President, Carter.

key fact Reagan, who became the new US President in 1980, was very anti-Communist and claimed that the USA had fallen behind the USSR in the nuclear arms race.

- Reagan doubled military expenditure, and pushed ahead with new weapons such as the **neutron bomb, Cruise, Pershing 2 and MX**. He also began the **Strategic Defence Initiative (SDI or 'Star Wars')**.

- As a result, disarmament talks (**START**) between the two superpowers broke down in 1985.

key fact However, in that year, Gorbachev became leader of the USSR.

- Gorbachev wanted to improve living standards and industrial efficiency and increase political freedom in the Soviet Union.

- He believed that attempting to keep up with US weapons developments was ruining the Soviet economy.

- As a result, he was determined not to follow the USA in Reagan's escalation of the arms race.

remember >>
Afghanistan had unofficially been accepted by the West as being in the 'Soviet sphere', given the shared borders.

B The closing stages

① key fact Gorbachev wanted to end this new arms race, and so decided to end the Cold War.

- Meetings took place between Gorbachev and Reagan in **Reykjavik in 1986** and in **Washington in 1987**.

- Gorbachev made such important concessions on nuclear weapons – basically accepting US superiority – that Reagan was forced to agree.

- The major agreements were:

  - The **Intermediate Nuclear Forces (INF) Treaty, 1987**, to reduce medium-range missiles.

  - The **Strategic Arms Reductions Talks (START) Treaty, 1991**, to reduce long-range missiles (made with Bush, who replaced Reagan in 1988).

- The two superpowers also agreed to reduce the conventional forces of NATO and the Warsaw Pact.

- Finally, Gorbachev ended Soviet intervention in Afghanistan.

remember >>

CIA reports showed that any Soviet attempt to match US developments would probably bankrupt its economy.

② key fact Gorbachev also announced that the USSR would no longer intervene in Eastern Europe to stop democratic reforms. This ended the Brezhnev Doctrine of 1968.

Gorbachev urged Eastern European governments to adopt the reforms he was making in the USSR (**perestroika**, **glasnost** and **demokratizatsiya**). From 1988 onwards, reforms took place and Soviet control ended.

remember >>

Although Gorbachev ended the Warsaw Pact, the USA refused to follow suit, so NATO continued in existence.

In Poland in 1989, Solidarity was legalised and won a majority in the elections.

In 1989, the Berlin Wall was knocked down.

In 1990, Germany was reunited.

The end of the Brezhnev Doctrine

In July 1991, the Warsaw Pact was dissolved.

③ key fact Gorbachev's policies were opposed by old-style Communists in the USSR.

- Economic problems and nationalist unrest increased their unease – in August 1991, they tried to overthrow him.

- Although the coup failed, the USSR ended in December after Russia formed the CIS with two other Soviet republics. The **Great Contest** and the Cold War were over.

>> practice questions

1 Why did Gorbachev decide not to keep up with the USA's development of new nuclear weapons?

2 What event finally led to the collapse of the USSR in December 1991?

McCarthyism and the Red Scare

- Although the USA and USSR had been allies during the Second World War, the capitalist USA had always been strongly opposed to Communism. These long-standing tensions resurfaced before the end of the war, and soon led to the start of the Cold War.

- Events such as the USSR ending the USA's monopoly of nuclear weapons, China's Communist Revolution in 1949 and the start of the Korean War in 1950 led to a 'Red Scare' in the USA.

- A leading role in this was played by Senator Joseph McCarthy, who, for a time, helped to create a witch-hunt against suspected Communists, including leading Hollywood actors and directors.

A Impact of the Cold War

>> key fact Ever since the Bolshevik Revolution in Russia in 1917, the USA had been strongly anti-Communist – even sending an army into Russia at the end of the First World War in an unsucessful attempt to topple the new Bolshevik government.

- **During the 1920s, there had been a Red Scare in the USA** – against trade unionists, socialists and anarchists, as well as Communists.

- Although the USA and the Soviet Union had been allies for a short time during the Second World War, old antagonisms soon flared up again after 1945, leading to the emergence of what became known as the **Cold War** – marked by the **Truman Doctrine** and the **Marshall Plan**.

- In particular, the US government and many US citizens were concerned about growing **Soviet influence and control in Eastern Europe**, and especially the **Berlin Crisis of 1948–9**.

- These fears increased after **China's Communist Revolution**, the ending of the **USA's monopoly of nuclear weapons** by the Soviet Union in 1949 and the **Korean War of 1950–3**.

remember >>

In July 1950, just after the Korean War began, Julius and Ethel Rosenberg were accused of passing atomic secrets to the USSR. Despite weak evidence, they were found guilty and executed in 1953.

B The Red Scare

>> key fact Such Cold War fears led the US government to set up the House Committee on Un-American Activities (HUAC) – this began to question people in order to discover Soviet agents.

- **The FBI also began to build up files** on anyone who might be a Communist or who might have links to Communists.

- **HUAC also widened its investigations into the Hollywood film industry** to see which actors, writers and directors might be Communists or Communist sympathisers.

- Some people used their rights to political beliefs and free speech under the United States Constitution to not give evidence to HUAC – particularly well known was the case of the **Hollywood Ten in 1947**. The Ten were eventually sentenced to between six and twelve months in prison.

- Loyalty Boards were set up to investigate government employees, and over two hundred people were forced to resign. **The McCarran Act** forced all Communist groups to register, banned Communists from certain jobs and denied them passports.

- In 1948, **Alger Hiss** was accused by HUAC of being a **Communist spy** – as his trial took place, the USSR exploded its first nuclear bomb. Hiss was sent to prison for five years for lying to the court.

remember >>

Supporters of the Hollywood Ten included the famous actors Humphrey Bogart and Lauren Bacall.

C McCarthy and McCarthyism

>> **key fact** The victory of the Chinese Communist Party in 1949, along with the Soviet Union exploding its first nuclear bomb, led to increased anti-Communist hysteria in the USA. One politician who whipped up this hysteria was Joseph McCarthy, the Republican Senator of Wisconsin.

- McCarthy claimed to have a list of **205 names of Communists working in the State Department**. Although he later altered his claims several times, the Senate set up a committee chaired by Senator Tydings to investigate Communists – **this anti-Communist witch-hunt became known as 'McCarthyism'**.

- At first, McCarthy got much support – **25 states brought in anti-Communist laws, and the media helped fuel the hysteria**. People, including teachers, lost their jobs and homes, and were even beaten up.

- **However, several on the Tydings Committee began to accuse McCarthy of being a fraud and said his charges were a hoax.** At first, McCarthy accused Senator Tydings of being a Communist sympathiser – and even used fake photographs to 'prove' his allegations.

- In 1953, Eisenhower, the new US President, set up a new committee to investigate – when McCarthy accused army officers of being Communist sympathisers, the media and the Senate turned against him. **In 1954, he was censured by the Senate.**

remember >>

Despite the decline of McCarthyism, HUAC continued its investigations and, in 1954, the Communist Party of the USA was officially banned.

>> practice questions

1   Name **one** international event in 1949 that contributed to fears about Communism in the USA.

2   Who were the Hollywood Ten?

The Civil Rights Movement, 1945–62

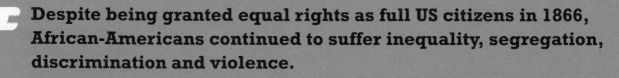

- Despite being granted equal rights as full US citizens in 1866, African-Americans continued to suffer inequality, segregation, discrimination and violence.

- From 1955, following the end of the Second World War, civil rights organisations were set up to campaign for an end to segregation in education and public facilities.

- Civil rights leaders, such as Martin Luther King, became involved in various peaceful protests. As the size of these civil rights movements grew, those opposed to civil rights for African-Americans became more violent.

A The position of African-Americans by 1945

>> **key fact** Although the Fourteenth Amendment to the United States Constitution in 1866 made African-Americans full US citizens, by 1945 they still faced racism, segregation, unequal treatment and violence – especially in the South.

- African-Americans were often prevented from voting, and many states in the South had racist laws – known as **Jim Crow laws** – to maintain **segregation and discrimination** in jobs, housing, education and healthcare.

- In many places, **whites and blacks were segregated across a range of facilities** – cafés, swimming pools, toilets, public transport, schools and healthcare.

remember >>

The public services and facilities available to blacks were usually worse than those for whites.

B The early Civil Rights Movement

>> **key fact** Before the Second World War, various organisations had been set up to campaign for equal and civil rights for blacks – the two main ones were the National Association for the Advancement of Colored People (NAACP) and the Congress of Racial Equality (CORE).

- After the Second World War, African-Americans hoped for greater equality and less racism and, although some whites changed their attitudes to working with blacks, most did not. **For most blacks, racism, segregation and inequality continued as before.**

- **This was especially true in the Southern states**, where their own state laws could only be overruled by the Supreme Court.

- Consequently, **more and more African-Americans joined civil rights organisations such as NAACP and CORE** or set up church-based groups. These groups often campaigned over different local issues.

- One of their main aims was to enforce the right of black people to vote.

- In the years 1945–51, the NAACP brought several cases to the Supreme Court to end segregation. In the early 1950s, the **NAACP supported the Brown vs. Board of Education** case to end segregation in schools. In 1954, the Supreme Court ruled that such segregation was unconstitutional – but no date was set for integration.

- Some schools did integrate – most did not. **White Citizens Councils** were set up in many parts of the South to prevent integration.

C Campaigns 1955–62

key fact Most early civil rights groups believed in peaceful protest and non-violent direct action, such as picketing, boycotts, sit-ins, freedom rides and mass marches.

- After 1955, **Martin Luther King** soon emerged as one of the main civil rights leaders. He first rose to prominence during the **Montgomery Bus Boycott in Alabama**, which began in December 1955.

- The Montgomery Bus Boycott was started by **Rosa Parks**, a member of the NAACP who refused to vacate a seat for a white person. The **Montgomery Improvement Association (MIA)** was set up to campaign against segregation on buses – Martin Luther King was its chairperson.

- The MIA organised a boycott of Montgomery's buses – most blacks **(who formed 70 per cent of the customers)** and some whites took part and, **after 381 days**, the bus company changed its policy.

- On 19 December 1956, the Supreme Court ruled **segregation on buses was unconstitutional**. Many whites in Montgomery and elsewhere were angry.

key fact Another important campaign of the early Civil Rights Movement was against the continued segregation of education.

- In 1957, the Central High School in Little Rock, Arkansas, attempted to integrate nine black students.

- However, Orville Faubus, the Governor of Arkansas, ordered the National Guard to keep them out. A mob of angry whites also gathered to prevent the black students gaining entrance.

- President Eisenhower sent in federal troops to enforce integration – Faubus just closed the school.

key fact The years 1960–1 also saw sit-ins and freedom rides. In Greensboro, North Carolina, sit-ins were organised to protest against segregated restaurants – and the Student Non-Violent Coordinating Committee (SNCC) was set up.

- In 1961, CORE and SNCC drove buses through the South to test that the Supreme Court ruling to desegregate facilities in bus stations was being carried out. These civil rights activists were called **Freedom Riders**. They often met violence, and three were killed – yet the protests continued.

>> practice questions

1 What do the initials CORE and SNCC stand for?

2 Who was Rosa Parks?

The Civil Rights Movement, 1963–75

- After 1961–2, civil rights campaigns continued – and violence against them increased.

- In 1963, important peace marches took place, with Martin Luther King playing a leading role – one result was the passing of important civil rights laws.

- However, some civil rights campaigners began to question the effectiveness of peaceful protest and, instead, began to support Black Power calls for more radical actions.

A Reactions to the civil rights campaigns

remember >>

A Freedom Riders' bus had been fire-bombed by a white mob at Anniston on 14 May 1961.

>> **key fact** The Ku Klux Klan (KKK), which used violence to suppress black civilians, had a membership that included judges, senior police officers and soldiers.

- The violence of whites who were opposed to the ending of segregation also led to a change in attitude of civil rights campaigners.

- Not only were they angry at the violence against Freedom Riders, they also grew increasingly frustrated at the **lack of federal government support for civil rights**.

- While Martin Luther King and others continued to support non-violent peaceful protest, others – such as the **Black Muslims and the Black Panthers** – began to consider more radical solutions and methods.

B 1963 and the peace marches

1 key fact Birmingham, Alabama, was notorious for its continuing segregation and for the number of bombings of houses, churches and businesses belonging to blacks – and for its chief of police, 'Bull' Connors, who was sympathetic to the KKK.

- In **1963**, civil rights campaigners decided to launch a large **non-violent desegregation campaign in Birmingham**.

- A series of marches took place – many were arrested, including Martin Luther King. Connors ordered the police to use **fire hoses and dogs against the marchers** – some blacks rioted in protest at this.

- **Media coverage** of these events led **President Kennedy to send in federal troops**. The mayor finally agreed to pass desegregation laws.

2 key fact The success of the Birmingham campaign led to other civil rights actions, although the violence continued. This led Congress to begin discussions about a civil rights bill.

- The Civil Rights Movement then decided on a **March on Washington in August 1963**. It was a massive protest, witnessing Martin Luther King's famous **'I have a dream'** speech.

C Results of the civil rights campaigns by 1965

>> **key fact** Kennedy appointed African-Americans to some key government jobs and set up committees to work out how to improve opportunities for black Americans.

- Although Kennedy had promised a new civil rights bill in June 1963, reforms were slow.

- **In the summer of 1964, SNCC decided to target Missisippi** – the most racist and segregated state in the USA.

- The main campaigners were white middle-class students – **they set up Freedom Schools and helped to train black Americans to pass voter registration**.

- However, they met great violence and six were killed – this created more publicity for the cause.

- In July 1964, Johnson, the new president, **pushed through the new Civil Rights Act.** This outlawed discrimination in all areas. In 1965, the **Voting Rights Act** was passed, allowing all blacks to register for the vote.

D Black Power and other civil rights groups

1 key fact Despite these gains, the violence continued into 1965. This eventually led to the emergence of other black leaders and groups.

- **The Nation of Islam** was one such group – its most famous member, until 1964, was **Malcolm X**.

- From 1965, riots swept the USA – often the result of police brutality and long-standing poverty.

- Another group was set up by **Stokely Carmichael** and other SNCC workers in Alabama – based on the ideas of **Black Power**.

- In October 1966, **Huey Newton** and **Bobby Seale** set up the **Black Panther Party** in California. By 1968, there were Black Panther groups in 25 US cities.

2 key fact Violence and riots continued in major cities during 1967 and 1968 – then, in April 1968, Martin Luther King was assassinated in Memphis, Tennessee.

- This led to hundreds of riots – it took over 500 000 soldiers to stop them and 46 people were killed.

- Following these riots, President Johnson set up the **Kerner Commission** – his report stressed that poverty and poor housing were largely responsible for the riots.

- Between 1968 and 1975, although discrimination continued in many areas, more blacks were able to get a **better education** and so get **better jobs**. Also, **blacks were elected to political office** and got other important reforms passed.

>> practice questions

1 **Who were the Freedom Riders?**

2 **When did Martin Luther King make his famous 'I have a dream' speech?**

Other inequalities and protests

 As well as African-Americans, other minority groups campaigned for equal rights during the period after the Second World War.

 These struggles for equal rights by ethnic groups inspired women to campaign in the 1960s and 1970s for equality and women's liberation.

 At the same time, the 1960s and 1970s also saw the rise of radical student protest groups.

A Other ethnic minority groups

>> **key fact** The struggles of African-Americans to obtain full civil rights inspired other ethnic minorities to mount their own campaigns.

- **Native Americans only became US citizens in 1924** – by 1945, serious problems of poverty, unemployment, poor education, alcoholism, depression and suicide still existed on their reservations.

- During the 1960s, Native Americans began to campaign for better treatment. As a result, **an act was passed by the US federal government in 1975**, giving compensation and new rights and powers of self-government to the reservations.

- **Hispanic-Americans** were another minority group who began to campaign for equality. They were mainly Spanish-speaking people from Mexico, Puerto Rico and Cuba.

B The Women's Liberation Movement

>> **key fact** During the Second World War, women had been encouraged to support the war effort by working in industry. However, after 1945, they were expected to return to housework and childcare.

- In the **1950s and 1960s**, most employers believed that women should not have serious 'career' jobs – **hence they got poor pay and few promotion prospects**. This was despite the fact that, from 1950 to 1960, the number of women at universities almost doubled.

- **In 1963, Betty Freidan's book** *The Feminine Mystique* drew attention to the dissatisfactions and ambitions of women. The same year, the Equal Pay Act was passed, while the **Civil Rights Act of 1964 made it illegal to discriminate on grounds of gender and race**. However, women still found it difficult to get equality.

- In 1966, Betty Freidan and others set up the **National Organisation for Women (NOW)** – a women's civil rights group – to secure political, professional and educational equality for women.

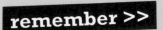
remember >>

A split took place in NOW over heterosexual marriage – some believed NOW should also campaign for equal rights for lesbians.

- Some, angered by the traditional female roles to which women in black civil rights groups were relegated, also challenged male chauvinist views of women – they went on to call for **women's liberation**. At first, they operated in local groups.

- These calls and protests led to much opposition – mostly from men. Even some radical political groups argued that women's liberation should take second place to other campaigns.

- Radical feminists resisted such calls, and continued the women's liberation campaigns.

- **In 1972, the Educational Amendment Act** banned gender discrimination in education, allowing girls to follow the same curriculum as boys. Women, however, were still less likely to get the highest-paying jobs.

- An attempt to get an Equal Rights Amendment (ERA) to the US Constitution failed. However, five women were elected to Congress in the early 1970s.

C The student movement

>> **key fact** The wave of protests in the 1960s also affected young people in general, especially students.

- Following the Second World War, **the US economy boomed and dominated the world** – partly because of huge government spending on the Cold War. As well as increased affluence, greater numbers of white middle-class youths were able to go to university.

- Many students wanted change in the 1960s – some set up an activist group called **Students for a Democratic Society (SDS)**. They organised protests and sit-ins over a range of issues, including poverty, civil rights and especially the Vietnam War.

- Although the right to vote was restricted to those aged 21 or over, **men as young as 17 were drafted (conscripted) into the armed forces to fight in Vietnam**.

- At first, protesters used **peaceful, non-violent methods** – but as the war in Vietnam escalated, and violence against black civil rights campaigners increased, some students (such as the Weathermen) began to call for a violent revolution.

- Many young men began to publicly **burn their draft cards or 'dodge the draft'** by leaving the USA. As the police response became more violent, some university students adopted stronger methods instead of relying on sit-ins, occupations and strikes.

- The worst violence was in **1970 at Kent State University in Ohio**, where large protests took place against the US invasions of Cambodia and Laos ordered by Nixon.

- The National Guard was called into the university to break up the protests. On 4 May 1970, it opened fire and **four students were killed**. After that incident, the SDS leadership began to break up.

>> practice questions

1 **When were Native Americans allowed to become US citizens?**

2 **Who was the main person behind the setting up of the National Organisation for Women (NOW) in 1966?**

The Liberal era begins

 When Queen Victoria died in 1901, Britain had an empire that covered 20 per cent of the world's land surface.

 However, many of Britain's 'old' or 'staple' industries (such as coal, iron and textiles) were facing increased competition from abroad.

 In 1906, the Liberals defeated the Conservatives (who had dominated British politics since 1886) and carried out several important reforms.

A Britain in 1900

1 key fact The empire provided British industry with raw materials and markets.

- Since 1875, Britain had been involved in the **Scramble for Africa**. This had brought it into conflict with France and the new state of Germany, formed in 1871.

- With high industrial production and exports, and the largest empire, Britain seemed the most powerful country in the world. The period 1901–14 became known as the **Golden Age**.

- However, **Germany, Japan and the USA** were rapidly becoming serious economic competitors. These countries put more money into modernising factories and developing newer industries such as chemicals and electrical goods.

2 key fact Despite Britain's great wealth, there was much poverty – especially in the industrial towns.

- Generally, however, real wages for most workers had improved since the 1880s, largely due to the **increase in trade unionism amongst unskilled and semi-skilled workers**.

- However, many employers wanted Parliament and the courts to limit successful strikes.

- The **Taff Vale Case in 1901** was a set-back for the unions, and came when prices were rising more quickly than wages. This led the unions to turn to Parliament.

- At first, many trade unionists supported the Liberals. However, in 1900, the TUC set up the **Labour Representation Committee (LRC)**, and this put pressure on the Liberals.

> **remember >>**
>
> The degree of poverty amongst the working class had been shown by the Boer War, 1899–1902, when many volunteers were rejected as unfit for military service.

B Liberal reforms, 1906–11

1 key fact In 1906, the Liberals won 377 seats, while 54 LRC MPs were also elected – about half of these were 'Lib-Labs'.

- Lib-Labs were working-class MPs who accepted the Liberal 'whip' but spoke freely on labour/working-class issues.

- There were also 83 Irish MPs who hoped to obtain **Home Rule for Ireland**, as this was supported by the Liberals.

- The Liberals, led by **Campbell-Bannerman**, were determined to push through social, political and industrial reforms.

- **Asquith** became Chancellor of the Exchequer, and **Lloyd George** became President of the Board of Trade. In 1908, Asquith became Prime Minister and Lloyd George took over as Chancellor.

key fact From 1906–09, a number of important acts were passed.

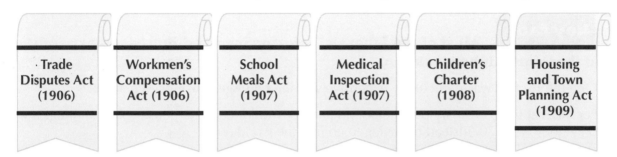

| Trade Disputes Act (1906) | Workmen's Compensation Act (1906) | School Meals Act (1907) | Medical Inspection Act (1907) | Children's Charter (1908) | Housing and Town Planning Act (1909) |

>> practice questions

Study Sources A and B below, which are about poverty in Britain in 1900, then answer the question that follows.

We have been used to looking upon the poverty in London as unusual [a survey by Booth in London in 1892 had shown that 30 per cent of the population lived below the poverty line]. However, the result of careful investigation shows that the proportion of poverty in London is practically equalled in what is a typical provincial town. We are faced with the startling probability that from 25–30 per cent of the urban population in the United Kingdom is living in poverty.

Source B: The conclusion reached by Rowntree, in *Poverty: a study of town life*, 1901. This was based on his research in York.

Source A: A slum in Sunderland at the beginning of the twentieth century

How far do Sources A and B agree about the extent of poverty in Britain at the beginning of the twentieth century?

Problems

- Some of the Liberal reforms were controversial and led to opposition from some sections of society, including the House of Lords.

- In addition, the Liberal government faced trouble from women's suffrage organisations, which demanded the right to vote.

A Opposition

1 key fact Most of the Liberals' reforms involved increased expenditure and therefore higher taxation.

- One reform that was particularly expensive was the **Old Age Pensions Act, 1908**.

- For the first time, ordinary people too old to work would receive a pension of 5 shillings a week once they were 70, instead of having to go into the workhouse.

2 key fact To pay for this, and other reforms, Lloyd George introduced the People's Budget in 1909.

The Budget mainly increased taxes on luxury items and the properties and incomes of the wealthiest people – but it also led to a **constitutional crisis**.

When the Budget went to the unelected House of Lords (where the Conservatives had a huge majority), it was rejected.

The Liberals called another election in January 1910, which they narrowly won.

The 1909 Budget was re-introduced – the Lords passed it this time, but rejected the Parliament Bill, which proposed **limiting the powers of the Lords**.

The Liberals called, and narrowly won, another election in December 1910 – they said if the Lords did not pass the bill, the King had agreed to create enough Liberal peers (lords) to cancel the Tory majority.

This made the Lords accept the bill. The **Parliament Act, 1911**, said the Lords could only delay a Budget for one month, and other bills for two years only – provided they were passed three times by the Commons.

remember >>

The January 1910 election result was close: the Liberals got 275 seats to the Tories' 273; Labour (with 40 seats) and the Irish Nationalists (82 seats) kept the Liberals in power.

B The Suffragists and Suffragettes

① key fact During the nineteenth century, men gradually won the right to vote. However, women remained without the vote.

- In **1897, the NUWSS** was set up by **Millicent Fawcett** – this used peaceful methods of protest. Members of the NUWSS were known as **Suffragists**.

- Reforms after 1870 gave women greater equality – including, in 1880 and 1894, the right to vote in local elections. **However, women were still excluded from voting in general elections.**

② key fact In 1903, the Pankhursts formed the WSPU. These Suffragettes were prepared to break the law in order to get the vote.

- The Liberals gave women the right to stand in county council elections in 1906, but not the right to vote in general elections.

- **From 1906, the WSPU became more militant** – they heckled ministers, chained themselves to railings and smashed windows. Many of those arrested refused to pay fines and were sent to prison.

- In prison, many women went on **hunger strike**. From 1909, they were **force-fed** – this led to a public outcry.

- In 1912, the WSPU campaign became more violent, including arson attacks on post boxes. **In 1913, Emily Davison was killed trying to stop the King's horse at the Derby.**

- In **1913**, the government passed the **Cat-and-Mouse Act**, which allowed prisoners on hunger strike to be released for a time – they would be put back in prison once their strength had been restored by food.

- However, when war broke out in 1914, the WSPU suspended its campaign.

remember >>

When the WSPU stepped up its campaign after 1910, the Liberals were also facing growing trouble in Ireland and large strikes in Britain.

>> practice questions

Study Source A below, then answer the question that follows.

Source A:
A poster against the force-feeding of Suffragettes, produced by the WSPU in 1910

exam tip >>

Make sure you use the source AND your own knowledge – don't do just one or the other.

How far do you trust this source for finding out about the treatment of Suffragettes in Britain in the years 1910–14? Explain your answer using the source and your own knowledge.

The reforms continue

- By 1912, the Liberal government was faced with a serious crisis in Ireland.

- Despite this, the Liberals continued with a programme of reforms.

- However, the outbreak of war in 1914 postponed these reforms, and the problem of Ireland.

A Ireland

1 key fact The Liberals had long supported some self-government for Ireland, but attempts to pass a Home Rule Act in 1886 and 1893 had failed.

- In the 1880s, some Irish Nationalists (led at first by Charles Stuart Parnell) had campaigned for Home Rule – self-government for Ireland in most, but not all, matters.

- Unlike the Liberals, the Conservatives were closely linked to the **Unionists** in Ireland, who wanted to remain **directly ruled by Britain**.

- When the Liberals won the election in 1906, the Irish **Nationalist** MPs (who supported Home Rule and were led by Redmond) expected the Liberals to introduce another Home Rule Bill.

- They helped the Liberals in their struggles with the Lords in 1910 and, in return, were promised Home Rule. Because the second election in 1910 was so close, their votes were crucial to the Liberals.

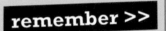

remember >>

At first, Home Rule was supported by both Catholics and Protestants.

2 key fact The Third Home Rule Bill was introduced in 1912 and passed through the Commons.

- Although the Lords rejected it, it would automatically become law in 1914 under the 1911 Parliament Act.

- Led by Sir Edward Carson, the Unionists – supported by some leading Conservatives, such as Lord Randolph Churchill (Winston Churchill's father) – formed a **Solemn League and Covenant in 1912** to resist Home Rule. They also set up the **Ulster Volunteer Force**, which soon had 100 000 armed members. Donations totalling over £1 million enabled them to buy weapons and begin military training.

- This worried the Nationalists and **Sinn Fein** party (set up in 1905). Those who wanted complete independence set up the **Irish Volunteers** – by 1914, they had 80 000 armed members. There was also the Irish Citizen Army, led by Connolly.

- **In 1914, the Curragh Mutiny** further alarmed the Nationalists – British army officers were allowed to resign their commissions temporarily rather than implement the new Home Rule Act. But then war broke out and the Home Rule Act was suspended until the end of the war.

B New Liberalism

① key fact After the 1910 elections, the Liberals became influenced by the more radical reforming ideas of what was known as New Liberalism.

- After 1910, the Liberals were dependent on the votes of Irish Nationalist and Labour Party MPs. They hoped New Liberalism would limit Labour's rise.

- In 1911, the Parliament Act gave salaries to MPs (Labour MPs had no private incomes), and the Trade Union Act made it easier for trade unions to make donations to political parties (overturning the 1909 Osborne judgement).

- The Liberals also passed acts to improve working conditions and pay (for example, for miners and shop workers).

- Especially important was the **1911 National Insurance Act**, which established sickness and short-term unemployment benefits for most workers. These were based on National Insurance contributions paid by workers, employers and the state.

- Although the Liberal government passed the Plural Voting Act in 1913, which stopped university graduates having two votes, women were still denied the vote.

② key fact The Liberals were also faced with a wave of huge strikes in 1910–12 – a time of unemployment and low pay.

- Violent confrontations between police and strikers took place – in some cases, the government sent in troops. Many ordinary trade unionists involved in these confrontations were influenced by 'syndicalist' ideas (anarchist beliefs that each industry should be controlled by those who worked in those industries).

- In 1913, the three biggest unions (the miners, the transport workers and the railway workers) formed the **Triple Industrial Alliance** to help workers against what they saw as cooperation between employers and the state.

- However, plans for a strike were called off when the war began in 1914.

> **remember >>**
>
> New Liberalism ideas and reforms helped begin a welfare state in Britain. The movement was influenced by reformers such as Booth and Beveridge. One supporter of this New Liberalism was Lloyd George.

>> practice questions

Study Source A, then answer the question that follows.

THE DAWN OF HOPE.

Mr. LLOYD GEORGE'S National Health Insurance Bill provides for the insurance of the Worker in case of Sickness.

Support the Liberal Government
in their policy of
SOCIAL REFORM.

Source A:
A poster about the National Insurance Act, issued by the government in 1911

> **exam tip >>**
>
> Make sure that you use your own knowledge to explain, and add to, what is in the source.

What can you learn about the National Insurance Act of 1911 from this source? Use the source and your own knowledge to explain your answer.

Winning minds

 When Britain declared war on Germany, thousands rushed to volunteer. But, as the war dragged on, the number of volunteers declined.

 To encourage men to enlist, the government produced propaganda about the Germans, and began to suppress bad news.

 Eventually, conscription was introduced to force men to join up.

A Recruitment and opposition

1 key fact When war broke out in August 1914, many thought it would be a short war ('over by Christmas').

- Others saw military service as a job – there were fewer volunteers in areas of low unemployment. **By September 1914, over 750 000 men had volunteered.**

- But the small **British Expeditionary Force (BEF)** sent over to help the French suffered heavy casualties. Some women (including the WSPU) encouraged men to enlist.

- The government began a campaign, headed by **Lord Kitchener**, to recruit 2.25 million men by October 1915.

- One method used was to create **Pals Battalions** by promising to keep together all volunteers from the same street, factory or town.

> **remember >>**
>
> The medically unfit and those in 'essential' war jobs (such as mining and farming) were exempt from conscription.

2 key fact However, as the war continued and the casualties grew, the number of volunteers declined. Compulsory conscription was therefore introduced in January 1916 by the Military Service Act.

CALL-UP CARD	**CALL-UP CARD**	**CALL-UP CARD**
Jan 1916	**March 1916**	**1918**
All single men aged 18–41	**Extended to married men**	**Extended to men up to 50**

3 key fact Some men refused to fight – these were conscientious objectors (known as conchies or COs).

- There were 16 000 COs – some objected to military service on religious or moral grounds, others on political grounds.

- Tribunals were set up to decide who were 'genuine' COs; most agreed to do non-combatant work at the front – these were known as **alternativists**.

- But about 1600 refused to do anything to help the war – these **absolutists** suffered harsh treatment in civilian and especially military prisons. After the war, all COs were denied the vote for five years.

B Propaganda

① key fact The government's secret War Propaganda Bureau drew up untrue or exaggerated stories about German atrocities.

These stories (for example, claiming that German troops ate Belgian babies, or used the corpses of British soldiers to make soap or cooking fats) were then **spread by the press**.

The purpose of these stories was to encourage more men to enlist, and to keep the civilian population supporting the war.

People began to attack Germans who lived in Britain and, in 1915, the government interned all German males aged 17–45. Older men, and women and children, were forced to move to Germany.

As well as government propaganda, bad news was also suppressed – for example, at first, the true number of casualties was often hidden, while successes were exaggerated.

remember >>

Anti-German feelings ran so high in Britain that, in 1917, the King changed his family's German surname (Saxe-Coburg-Gotha) to Windsor.

② key fact In 1917, the National War Aims Committee was set up to hold rallies and issue leaflets to keep up civilian morale.

One aim of the Committee was to create an atmosphere in which any anti-war sentiments would be deeply unpopular.

People who tried to tell the truth – even soldiers – were punished, and often beaten up by those influenced by such propaganda.

Poster campaigns were launched to make civilians feel part of the war effort – for example, asking people to eat less or to do essential war work.

>> practice questions

Study Source A below, then answer the question that follows.

I believe that the war is being prolonged by those who have the power to end it. I believe the war upon which I entered as a war of defence and liberation has now become a war of conquest and aggression. I have seen and endured the sufferings of the troops and I can no longer be a party to prolong these sufferings for ends which I believe to be evil and unjust.

Source A:
Part of 'A soldier's declaration', written by Siegfried Sassoon in July 1917. Sassoon was a famous English poet, and served as an infantry officer during the First World War.

exam tip >>

You need to consider the provenance of the source.

How useful is this source as historical evidence of the amount of opposition to the war? Use the source and your own knowledge to explain your answer.

The home front (1)

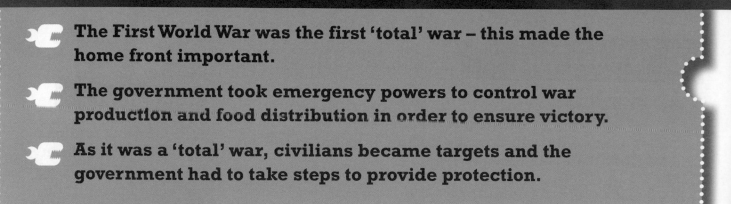

- The First World War was the first 'total' war – this made the home front important.

- The government took emergency powers to control war production and food distribution in order to ensure victory.

- As it was a 'total' war, civilians became targets and the government had to take steps to provide protection.

A DORA

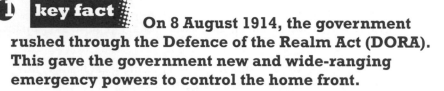

① key fact On 8 August 1914, the government rushed through the Defence of the Realm Act (DORA). This gave the government new and wide-ranging emergency powers to control the home front.

- Later that month, another DORA was passed, which increased those powers. **The government began to get involved in the economy and people's lives** more than ever before.

- **DORA had four main aims.**

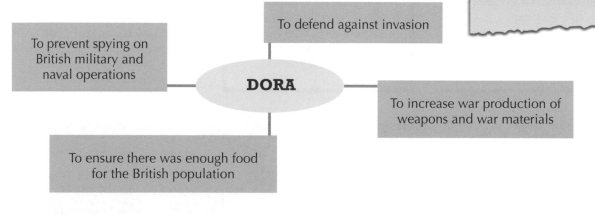

To defend against invasion

To prevent spying on British military and naval operations

DORA

To increase war production of weapons and war materials

To ensure there was enough food for the British population

② key fact DORA allowed the government and the military to censor newspaper reports and films (via the Department of Information), along with letters sent home by soldiers.

- DORA also banned people from discussing military matters in public or spreading rumours. Even the sale of binoculars and the ringing of church bells (unless Britain was being invaded) were banned.

- It also made it illegal to use invisible ink when writing letters abroad.

- At first, DORA allowed for imprisonment without trial – but trial by jury was restored in 1915.

③ **key fact** DORA allowed the government to take over any factory or workplace for war production.

- A special **Ministry of Munitions** was set up to control weapons production. The government also took over the running (but not ownership) of ship-building, mining, transport and the railways.

- To boost production, **British Summer Time** was introduced, giving an extra hour of daylight for farm workers and others.

- However, the strain of long hours – and employers who tried to keep wages low – led to a number of strikes, which meant losses in production.

B Civilians as targets

>> **key fact** As the First World War was a 'total' war, the front line shifted to the home front, with attempts to break civilian morale in two main ways.

Shelling

- In November 1914, Great Yarmouth, on the Norfolk coast, was the first British town to be shelled by German ships.

- In December, three other east-coast towns were shelled – in Scarborough, 19 people died and 80 were injured.

Air-raids

- However, from 1915, naval attacks were replaced by air raids. In January, King's Lynn and Great Yarmouth in Norfolk were the first British towns to be bombed from Zeppelins.

- Zeppelins were huge airships filled with hydrogen gas. Underneath was a cabin from which the crew dropped bombs – 20 Zeppelin raids on London killed 188 people. In all, almost 2000 civilians were killed or injured in 51 Zeppelin raids on Britain from 1915 to 1918.

- Britain took effective steps to counter the Zeppelins – searchlights, barrage (barrier) balloons, incendiary bullets and night-fighters.

- DORA allowed local military authorities to impose a 'blackout' – this forced people to put out all lights if an air raid was expected. By the end of 1916, the government had also recruited over 17 000 people to protect civilians.

- So, in 1917, the Germans switched to Gotha IV bomber planes – these killed or injured almost 3000 civilians in 57 raids. In one raid on London, 162 were killed.

- There was great fear of bombing raids. Many sheltered in the London Underground – or in caves in Dover (the town that suffered most bomber attacks).

remember >>

Air raids (whether by Zeppelins or bombers) failed to destroy civilian morale, despite almost five thousand deaths.

>> practice questions

1 **List the four main aims of DORA.**

2 **Describe the methods used by DORA to increase war production.**

The home front (2)

- Another serious problem on the home front were the food shortages caused by the German U-boat campaign.

- These almost led to defeat, but were eventually overcome.

- This problem (as with air raids) fell mainly on women, who also played major roles in the war effort.

A Rationing

① key fact
There were serious food shortages in Britain as a result of the increasing attacks by German U-boats (submarines) on merchant shipping.

- Even in 1914, there was an awareness that food should not be wasted: DORA made it illegal to feed bread to chickens, horses and dogs.

- But by 1916, 4 per cent of British shipping and neutral ships trading with Britain were being sunk by German U-boats, and serious food shortages began to hit Britain.

- In **1917**, the government introduced **voluntary rationing** in order to reduce food consumption and distribute what there was more equally.

- People were asked to eat no more than 340 grams of sugar, 1.8 kilograms of bread and 1.1 kilograms of meat a week.

- But this failed, as poor people could not even afford to buy the amounts of sugar and meat permitted; while rich people simply bought extra on the 'black market'.

- Then, in 1917, the German U-boat campaign was stepped up – by April 1917, it was claimed that Britain had only six weeks' food supply left.

> **remember >>**
>
> Despite the fact that rationing improved the diets of many ordinary people, for others the reduced intake of food left them vulnerable to the flu epidemic of 1918 – almost 230 000 British people died.

② key fact
So, in 1918, full-scale compulsory rationing was introduced.

- Because this new system worked reasonably well, the diets of many poor people were better than they had been in 1914.

- Under DORA, the government also had the power to take over any land it needed in order to increase food production. In particular, it turned public parks and other unused land into fields and allotments to grow extra food.

- **Between 1914 and 1918, over 1.2 million hectares of such land were taken over.** But the food shortages continued.

- Lord Devonport became Food Controller and organised a successful increase in wheat and potato production.

B The role of women

① key fact With so many men at the front, serious labour shortages arose – these gaps were filled by women.

- Especially important were those who worked in munitions (armaments) factories. There were about 900 000 **munitionettes** by 1918.

- During the 1915 'shell shortage' crisis, Lloyd George financed a march led by Mrs Pankhurst that called on employers to take on more women workers.

- Many women worked in engineering factories, or became conductors on trams and buses, while over 400 000 became clerks and secretaries. Before 1914, these had been mainly male occupations.

- Many other women joined the **Women's Land Army** to do farm work.

② key fact Other women did various jobs more directly related to the military effort.

Voluntary Aid Detachments (VADs)	Women's jobs	Women's military units formed in 1917–18 , such as the **WAAC**, **WRNS** or **WRAF**.
Most VAD jobs were traditional women's jobs, such as laundresses, cooks, maids and nurses.	First Aid Nursing Yeomanry (FANY)	Most acted as cooks or clerks.
	Some acted as **ambulance drivers** or **motorbike messengers** at the front.	Some became **drivers** or **welders**.

remember >>

Many women, including the Suffragettes, campaigned for men to enlist.

- At the end of the war, most women lost their jobs (Pre-War Practices Act, 1919) and returned to their traditional roles.

- However, **in 1918, women over the age of 30 were, at last, given the vote.**

>> practice questions

Study Source A, then answer the questions that follow.

Source A: A female bus conductor, London, 1917

1 Explain why some women issued 'white feathers' to young men.

2 Explain why large numbers of women became employed in a wider variety of jobs during the First World War.

3 How far was women's status in society changed by the war?

exam tip >>

Think of several reasons for each answer, not just one.

Impact of the First World War

> The First World War led to huge debts for Britain, as well as having a negative effect on trade and industry.

> There were some reforms after the war, but economic problems led to industrial unrest.

A Economic and social problems

1 **key fact** By 1918, Britain had a debt of £10 billion, and much trade had been lost, especially to the USA and Japan.

- This resulted in a **large balance of payments deficit** (that is, imports cost more money than exports brought in).

- Long-term problems for many British industries were made worse by the war, especially in the **staple industries of coal, iron and steel**.

- After the war, there was increased competition from abroad. By 1920, loss of wartime contracts and demobilisation had resulted in a slump. **By 1921, there were over two million unemployed.**

- To deal with this long-term unemployment, an **Unemployment Insurance Act in 1921** allowed payment of uninsured benefit – this was known as the **dole**.

- To pay for this, the Unemployment Fund was allowed to borrow £30 million from the Treasury. Later acts, in 1927 and 1929, reduced benefits and their duration.

remember >>

To pay for the war, Britain doubled income tax, introduced several new indirect taxes, raised loans and sold almost 25 per cent of overseas assets. 75 per cent of spending had gone on the war.

2 **key fact** Before the war, Lloyd George had promised soldiers a 'fit country for heroes' as mass conscription had revealed poor diets, bad housing and lack of education.

Education Act, 1919, raised school-leaving age to 14 and set up medicals for older children.

Addison Housing Act, 1919, planned to build 200 000 new 'council' houses to replace slums.

Women over 30 received the vote in 1918 and the right to stand as MPs.

- During the war, many workers had benefited from government control of wages, prices and industry.

- In 1919–20, several strikes won wage rises that kept pace with prices. However, the post-war slump made employers keen to regain control of their companies and reduce wages.

remember >>

Although trade revived a little in the years after the war, unemployment did not drop below one million before 1939.

B The coal industry

>> **key fact** Particular problems existed in coal mining. Although, after the war, the majority of a Commission of Inquiry recommended nationalisation (government ownership), the government instead decided to end government control in March 1921.

- The mine owners immediately announced **wage cuts**. A planned Triple Industrial Alliance strike for 15 April failed when the railway workers withdrew (**Black Friday**).

- Another serious crisis hit in 1925 – again, the mine owners demanded wage cuts, along with an increase in the working day.

- The Triple Industrial Alliance was revived but, in July, the government gave the mine owners a subsidy (to last until April 1926) to prevent the wage cuts (**Red Friday**).

- The Samuel Commission was set up but, at the same time, the government made plans for dealing with a major strike – including the use of troops, and the setting up of the semi-official Organisation for the Maintenance of Supplies (OMS) to recruit people to act as **scabs**, or strike-breakers.

- When the subsidy ended, the owners insisted on the wage cuts. The miners persuaded the Trades Union Congress (TUC) to call a general strike in May, but they called it off after only nine days. In part, this was because in many areas, workers had come out on strike before the date set by the TUC. Also, in several towns strikers had gone beyond TUC instructions and had taken control of transport and the distribution of food and even organised workers' defense groups to protect strikers from the police and the OMS.

- The **Trade Disputes Act 1927** made all general and 'sympathy' strikes illegal, and many strikers were sacked.

remember >>

High rates of unemployment meant it was difficult to stage successful strikes, as there were always people desperate enough to take the place of any strikers.

>> practice questions

Study Source A below, then answer the questions that follow.

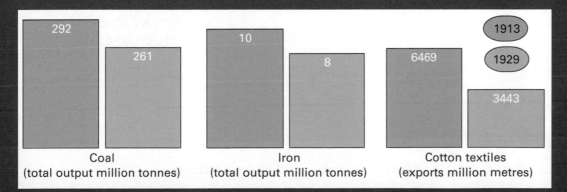

Source A: Chart showing the decline of staple industries in Britain, 1913–29

	1913	1929
Coal (total output million tonnes)	292	261
Iron (total output million tonnes)	10	8
Cotton textiles (exports million metres)	6469	3443

1 Explain what you understand by the term 'staple industries'.

2 By how much, according to the source, did exports of British textiles decline in the period 1913–29?

3 Give two reasons to explain why the British economy was in decline during the 1920s.

Political and economic problems

- As well as industrial decline and unrest, Britain faced other political and economic problems before 1939.

- Particularly important issues were Ireland and the start of the Great Depression.

A Ireland

1 **key fact** Many Irishmen (Catholic and Protestant) joined the army when the First World War began in 1914.

- However, a minority of Republicans (who wanted more than was offered by the Home Rule Act of 1914) saw the war (and the postponement of the Act) as **an opportunity for gaining complete independence**.

- In Dublin, on Easter Monday 1916, about 2000 Irish Volunteers and members of the Irish Citizen Army took over important buildings and proclaimed the independence of Ireland.

- After six days of fighting, the survivors of the **Easter Rebellion** surrendered – 15 were executed for treason.

2 **key fact** This turned the rebels into national heroes.

In the 1918 elections, Sinn Fein won 73 out of Ireland's 105 seats. Led by de Valera, they set up their own parliament (Dail Eireann).

A guerrilla 'war of independence' then began between the IRA and the British army. The British sent a force of 10 000 special troops (mainly unemployed ex-soldiers) – the officers were known as the **Auxiliaries**, and the ordinary soldiers as the **Black and Tans** (because of their mixed use of police and army uniforms).

As a result, the fighting continued but, in 1921, stalemate led to a truce.

In **1920**, Britain passed the **Government of Ireland Act**, dividing Ireland into **Northern Ireland** and the **Irish Free State** in the south. This was accepted by the Unionists in the north, but not by Sinn Fein.

remember >>

The IRA was the Irish Republican Army, set up by Sinn Fein after it declared independence following its victory in the 1918 elections. It was first led by Michael Collins.

3 **key fact** A majority of Sinn Fein accepted the partition of Ireland in 1922.

- However, a minority (led by de Valera) rejected it. A civil war then broke out between the pro- and anti-Treaty groups, which was won by the pro-Treaty forces in 1923.

- De Valera's Fianna Fail won the 1932 elections. He began to reduce British powers, and in **1937** the south was renamed **Eire**.

The start of the Depression

①  key fact
After the General Strike of 1926, the British economy benefited from an improvement in world trade and unemployment dropped to one million.

- In **1929**, the Labour Party won the largest number of seats (for the first time). **MacDonald** was the prime minister of this second minority government.

- However, when the **Wall Street Crash** in the USA triggered off the Great Depression, British exports fell by almost 50 per cent and unemployment rose to over three million.

- Although more had to be paid out in unemployment benefits, tax revenues began to decline as so many people were now without jobs.

② key fact
By 1931, Britain was in a serious economic crisis.

- Early suggestions to help the unemployed were opposed by Treasury civil servants and the Conservatives.

- When the USA called in loans it had made to Germany, Britain lent Germany (and Austria) £200 million to prevent their total collapse, which would have hit British exports further.

③ key fact
In 1931, MacDonald set up the May Committee to report on the crisis and make suggestions, as his earlier steps had been criticised by many people.

- The Committee's report recommended huge cuts in benefits, the wages of public servants and government spending.

- The USA, which had already loaned Britain £100 million, refused to lend more until huge cuts in government spending were made.

> **remember >>**
> Thirty million pounds were borrowed to pay unemployment benefits.

>> practice questions

Study Source A, then answer the questions that follow.

Source A: Two Black and Tan soldiers search a suspected Sinn Fein supporter. Another Sinn Fein suspect lies dead in the road.

1 Briefly explain why the special British troops known as the 'Black and Tans'.

2 What can you learn from Source A about the methods used by the Black and Tans during the war in Ireland in the years 1919–21?

Britain in the 1930s

- Unemployment was the biggest problem in Britain after 1931.

- However, disagreements in the Labour Party led to the formation of a new government.

- The new government's measures were not very popular, especially those dealing with unemployment benefits.

A Formation of the National Government

1 key fact MacDonald, the Labour Prime Minister, and Snowden, the Chancellor, agreed to the cuts recommended by the May Committee, including a ten per cent cut in unemployment benefit.

- Most Labour ministers, and the Labour Party, were opposed to these cuts.

- MacDonald resigned, but instead of a new election being called, the King asked MacDonald to form a coalition **National Government**, to include leading members of the other two parties.

2 key fact MacDonald agreed to lead this new National Government. It was supported by the whole of the Conservative Party and most of the Liberal Party. However, the Labour Party and most of its MPs were against it – they now became the Opposition.

remember >>

MacDonald and his Labour supporters in the Commons were seen as traitors for agreeing to form a government with the Conservatives, and were later expelled from the party.

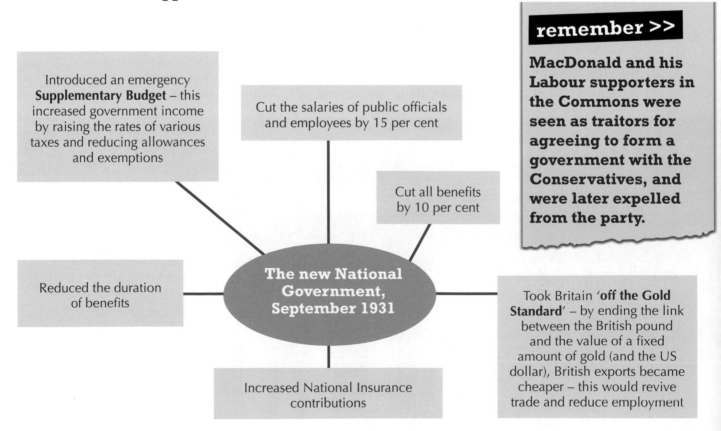

Introduced an emergency **Supplementary Budget** – this increased government income by raising the rates of various taxes and reducing allowances and exemptions

Cut the salaries of public officials and employees by 15 per cent

Cut all benefits by 10 per cent

Reduced the duration of benefits

The new National Government, September 1931

Took Britain 'off the Gold Standard' – by ending the link between the British pound and the value of a fixed amount of gold (and the US dollar), British exports became cheaper – this would revive trade and reduce employment

Increased National Insurance contributions

B The National Government in action

>> key fact
In October 1931, MacDonald called an election – the National Government won a big majority, but most were 'National' Conservative MPs. This new government had three main policies for dealing with the Depression.

remember >>

The National Government became increasingly dominated by Conservatives. After the 1935 election, which the National Government won with a reduced majority, MacDonald resigned and was replaced by Stanley Baldwin, the Conservative leader. In 1937, Neville Chamberlain became Prime Minister.

Protectionism	State subsidies	The unemployed
• The National Government put higher import duties (tariffs) on some foreign products (known as 'protectionism', as it tried to protect British manufacturers from foreign competition). • However, Snowden, the Chancellor, feared other countries would retaliate and so hit British exports even more. He resigned and was replaced by Neville Chamberlain (a Conservative). • In 1932, Chamberlain brought in the Import Duties Act, which put a 10 per cent duty on all foreign goods.	• In 1932, the National Government gave state subsidies to railway companies and financed public work schemes in the most distressed areas. • This aid was increased by the Depressed Areas Act, 1934, which spent about £2 million a year in these 'special areas'. In 1934, Chamberlain reduced income tax.	• In 1934, the Unemployment Insurance Act set up the Unemployment Assistance Board to deal with extra payments to the unemployed. Although the 1931 benefit cuts were partly reversed, a means test was introduced. • The unemployed resented this – in the worst hit areas, there were **hunger marches**. The most famous was the **Jarrow Crusade of 1936**.

Study Sources A and B below, then answer the question that follows.

A definite increase in malnutrition is shown for 1932 and 1933. The economic depression has undoubtedly lowered the standard of living in many homes and has contributed to the above increase, partly directly, but mainly by aggravating other causes of malnutrition.

Source A: An extract from the Report of the Schools Medical Officer, Carmarthen, South Wales, 1932–3

I have here a budget made out for me by an unemployed miner and his wife. I asked them to make a list which represented as exactly as possible their expenditure in a typical week. This man's allowance was 32 shillings a week, and besides his wife he had two small children... The basis of their diet, therefore, is white bread and margarine, corned beef, sugared tea, and potatoes. The results of all this are physical degeneracy.

Source B: An extract from *The Road to Wigan Pier*, 1937, by the English novelist and journalist, George Orwell

exam tip >>

Remember to make detailed references to BOTH sources.

How far do Sources A and B agree about the effects of the Great Depression in Britain in the 1930s?

Britain and the start of the war

- Even before the war began, some steps (such as conscription) had already been taken.

- Lessons from the First World War (especially the importance of retaining skilled workers) were also applied.

- At the same time, similar steps were taken on censorship and propaganda.

A Recruitment

① key fact Because of the growing threat posed by Nazi Germany after the Czech crisis of September 1938, Britain had already begun to make war preparations.

In March 1939, after Nazi Germany's invasion of the rest of Czechoslovakia, **Britain and France had signed a treaty with Poland.**

In April 1939, the British government introduced conscription – **the first time this had ever been done in peacetime**. The Military Training Act called up men aged 20–21.

In September 1939, the **Call-up** was extended to all men aged 19–41 – later widened to include 18-year-olds. However, in the early stages, the Call-up was criticised for being slow. Over one million men volunteered for military service, or asked for their Call-up to be speeded up.

remember >>

Many of those who rushed to volunteer believed that fascism was an evil that had to be fought, and had been highly critical of appeasement.

② key fact There was a more thought-out system of recruitment than in the previous war.

- A **Schedule of Reserved Occupations** had been drawn up, and employers in war-related industries could ask for the Call-up of specialist workers to be deferred.

- This system avoided the skilled labour shortages that had caused problems at the start of the First World War.

- In 1940, after the evacuation of the BEF from Dunkirk, the fear of invasion increased. Men who had not been called up were recruited into the **Local Defence Volunteers** (set up in May 1939).

- By the end of June 1940, there were over 1.5 million volunteers. In July, they were renamed the **Home Guard**. Their job was to help prevent a German invasion by guarding the coasts, setting up roadblocks and protecting telephone exchanges. However, their weapons were limited and mostly old.

B Propaganda and censorship

> **key fact** As in the First World War, the British government used censorship and propaganda to safeguard military information and to keep up civilian morale.

Censorship

 The **Censorship Bureau** banned all newspaper photographs of wounded soldiers, dead air-raid victims and houses destroyed by enemy bombing.

 Because of spies, the government ran poster campaigns such as the 'Careless Talk Costs Lives' campaign.

 However, the radio broadcasts by 'Lord Haw-Haw' from Nazi Germany were not banned, and the BBC was not taken over.

Propaganda

 The government ran poster campaigns to make everyone feel they were part of the war effort – such as 'Your Britain. Fight For It Now', 'Is Your Journey Really Necessary?' and 'Dig For Victory'. Churchill and other ministers made regular radio broadcasts urging people to 'do their bit'.

 The **Ministry of Information** also issued propaganda to help maintain morale. Particularly important was how it turned the defeat at **Dunkirk** into a 'victory' – soon everyone was talking about the 'Dunkirk spirit'. During the **Battle of Britain**, German aircraft losses were exaggerated.

remember >>

Music and comedy radio programmes helped keep up morale. Cinemas showed films of Britons working to win the war, Allied successes and glorified British victories from the past.

Study Sources A and B below, then answer the questions that follow.

We want large numbers of men between the ages of 17 and 65 to come forward now and offer their services in order to make assurances that an invasion will be repelled. The name of the new force will be the Local Defence Volunteers.

Source A: Anthony Eden, the British Secretary of State for War, speaking on the radio in May 1939

Source B: The Home Guards

1 What nickname was given to the LDVs/Home Guard?

2 Describe the key roles undertaken by these men during the war.

The war at home

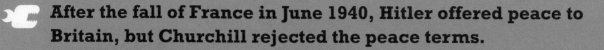

- After the fall of France in June 1940, Hitler offered peace to Britain, but Churchill rejected the peace terms.

- This led to the Battle of Britain – Hitler's first step in the planned invasion of Britain.

- As well as Germany's attempt to destroy the RAF and so win control of the skies, it also made civilians targets in what became known as 'the Blitz'.

A The Battle of Britain

1 key fact When Churchill refused to make peace in June 1940, Hitler ordered the invasion of Britain – Operation Sealion.

- The first stage of this **Battle of Britain** began in July 1940, when the German Luftwaffe bombed merchant shipping in the Channel.

- In August, in an attempt to **gain control of the skies**, they tried to destroy radar stations, airfields and RAF Fighter Command.

- Hitler also ordered the bombing of British industrial and shipping centres.

- The RAF fought back and, at first, was able to offer an effective response. But, by early September, the RAF's losses were greater than the numbers of new planes being produced.

- Then, just at the critical moment – and following an RAF bombing raid on Berlin – Hitler ordered the Luftwaffe to begin the night bombing of London – this was the start of **the Blitz**.

2 key fact By the time the Luftwaffe resumed its attacks on Fighter Command, the RAF was in a much stronger position, as the factories had produced almost 2000 fighters in four months.

- Large numbers of German bombers and fighters were destroyed and, in the end, the Luftwaffe failed to win control of the skies.

- Government propaganda exaggerated the number of German planes destroyed during the Battle of Britain. It also greatly emphasised the role of the Spitfire in the battle when, in fact, the RAF used the Hurricane much more.

- At the end of September 1940, Hitler postponed his plans for the invasion of Britain. From then until June 1941, Britain was without an ally.

- Although the bombing raids declined after 1941, new dangers emerged in 1944 and 1945 – these were the **V1** and **V2** attacks. But damage to factories was limited, and the attacks did little to slow vital war production.

remember >>

Other major cities were also bombed during the Blitz, not just London. They included Liverpool, Norwich, Manchester and Plymouth.

B   The Blitz

key fact **The British government was greatly concerned about the possible impact of bombing raids on civilian morale. This fear of bombing had contributed to the policy of appeasement.**

Gas masks – issued during the Czechoslovak crisis in 1938 and again when war was declared

Barrage balloons

Anti-aircraft batteries

Official air-raid shelters (the **Anderson** and the **Morrison**) – by 1945, over two and a half million had been provided

Government steps to protect the public

Air-Raid Precautions (ARP) wardens – recruitment began in 1937 and, by 1939, there were almost 500 000. They patrolled the streets, enforced the **blackout regulations**, helped people to shelters and gave help after air raids.

Searchlights

key fact **The first air raids of the Blitz began in September 1940, when London was bombed. They continued until May 1941.**

- Apart from docks, factories and railways, civilian housing was also targeted.

- In London, many people occupied the Underground stations. In other cities, people trekked out to the countryside each night, but most used the official shelters.

- In all, over 60 000 civilians were killed in the Blitz, and over 250 000 homes destroyed.

- Although there was some loss of morale at first, most were determined to resist.

Study Sources A and B below, then answer the questions that follow.

Source A: A photograph showing the delivery of Anderson shelters

After a heavy air raid there was the task of piecing the bodies together in preparation for burial. The stench was the worst thing about it – that and having to realise that these frightful pieces of flesh had once been living, breathing people. It became a grim satisfaction when a body was reconstructed – but there were always odd limbs which did not fit and there were too many legs. Unless we kept a firm grip on ourselves nausea was inevitable.

Source B: An aspect of the Blitz of 1940, as remembered by a first-aid worker

1   Briefly explain what Anderson shelters were, as shown in Source A.

2   What can you learn from these sources about the impact of the Blitz on civilians?

Women and the 'double burden'

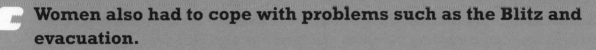

- As in the First World War, there were problems with food rationing – with so many men away because of the war, this particularly affected women.

- Women also had to cope with problems such as the Blitz and evacuation.

- Finally, women also played key roles in war production and defence organisations.

A Evacuation and rationing

1 key fact The British government evacuated children from high-risk bombing areas. In September 1939, about 1.5 million children were evacuated, along with some mothers, pregnant women and teachers.

- However, almost 50 per cent of parents kept their children at home. During the **Phoney War** (September 1939 to April 1940), many other parents brought their evacuated children home.

- Once the Blitz started, though, evacuation began again – by 1941, over three million had been evacuated.

2 key fact As in the last war, German U-boat attacks led to food shortages. Until 1943, British merchant shipping losses were very high, and food imports were down by 50 per cent.

- In January 1940, **rationing began** of those foods in short supply.

- People registered with their usual shops, and were given ration books – these had **coupons** to exchange for set amounts of foods.

- At the end of 1941, all tinned foods were rationed.

3 key fact The government also ran campaigns to increase food production and avoid waste.

- The **Dig for Victory** campaign encouraged people to dig up lawns and parks – by the end of 1942, the number of allotments had doubled to almost 1.5 million.

- Soap, shoes and clothes were also rationed, and there was a **Make Do and Mend** campaign.

- The use of petrol was discouraged by the **Is Your Journey Really Necessary?** campaign.

remember >>

Food supplies improved when Germany began to lose the Battle of the Atlantic.

B Women and the war effort

1 **key fact** Women played a big role in the war effort.

In September 1939, women were encouraged to volunteer for one of the women's sections of the armed forces, or to do essential war work.

In 1941, all single women aged **19–30 were conscripted** and had to choose one of those options.

By 1943, over seven million women were involved, and over 50 per cent of women aged 14–59 did some form of war service.

This, plus government control of 75 per cent of industry, resulted in industrial production being eight times higher in 1943 than in 1939.

remember >>

Women coped with war-time pressures as well as working in agriculture, industry, defence or the armed forces – this is called the 'double burden'.

2 **key fact** Many women worked in munitions factories or those producing other vital war supplies.

- Many others drove lorries and buses, or worked on the railways.

- About 30 000 women were in the **Women's Land Army**, doing agricultural work. Others worked in offices, especially the civil service and the Post Office.

- There were also about 500 000 women in the three women's armed services.

- While most did office work or acted as drivers, some **ATA** members flew newly produced planes from the factories to air bases, while some **WRNS** radio mechanics flew to test new equipment.

- Women in the **ATS** also worked on anti-aircraft batteries. Others worked as nurses.

remember >>

Some women in the Special Operations Executive (SOE) took part in combat.

>> practice questions

Study Sources A and B below, then answer the question that follows.

Source A: Members of the Women's Land Army during the Second World War

Source B: SOE agents, including a woman, receiving 'instinctive firing' training

Briefly explain the key roles played by women in the Second World War. Use the sources and your own knowledge to explain your answer.

Labour's Welfare State

 In July 1945, with the Second World War still being fought against Japan, Labour won a landslide victory in the general election, defeating the Conservatives, who were led by Winston Churchill.

 This new Labour government was committed to a range of new policies, including the creation of a free National Health Service and a better welfare state.

 The other main objective was to nationalise parts of British industry to reconstruct war-damaged Britain.

A The 1945 election

>> **key fact** When a general election was called for in July 1945, many assumed that Winston Churchill, the war-time prime minister in charge of a coalition government, would win. But the actions of Conservative governments during the 1930s (e.g. the Depression and Appeasement) still angered many, while the struggle against fascism and the war had radicalised others – including many in the armed forces.

- The Labour Party was, in part, a **socialist party** and **Clause 4 of its constitution** committed the party to create a fairer and more equal society by a redistribution of wealth – to be achieved partly via the **nationalisation of industry** (i.e. moving from private to state or public ownership).

- The Labour Party had also strongly committed itself to carrying out the recommendations of the **Beveridge Report of 1942**. This included tackling the **'five giants' of Want, Disease, Ignorance, Squalor and Idleness**, which needed to be addressed to wipe out poverty and create a more healthy and equal society. The Conservatives had been less prepared to accept these recommendations.

> **remember >>**
>
> Before 1945, both Liberal and Conservative governments had created some nationalised industries – not for socialist reasons, but for the practical needs of a modern and efficient economy.

B Beveridge and the Welfare State

>> **key fact** During the Second World War, medical care had been provided whether people could pay or not. In 1942, the Beveridge Report had recommended setting up a permanent free health service, including hospital and specialist services.

- The new Labour government was fully committed to the idea of a national health service for all. It was to cover all aspects of health care – and its introduction was to be overseen by **Aneurin Bevan, the Minister for Health**.

- To achieve this, he had to overcome **fierce opposition from many doctors**, who feared loss of income from private medicine and a reduction of their professional independence.

- Most doctors were won over by promises that they could continue private work once they had done some work for the National Health Service (NHS). So, on **5 July 1948, the NHS came into existence**.

- However, **in 1949**, as a result of an economic crisis, a completely free health service was ended when **some small charges for prescriptions were introduced**.

C Nationalisation

>> key fact Socialists in the Labour Party had, in 1918, succeeded in getting Clause 4 into the party's constitution. This committed a Labour government to taking important parts of industry and banking into common (i.e. public) ownership.

- In fact, by 1945, some government-owned (i.e. nationalised) industries and public utilities had already been set up by previous Liberal and even Conservative governments, such as the Central Electricity Generating Board (CEGB), the British Broadcasting Corporation (BBC) and the British Overseas Airways Corporation (BOAC).

- This had been done because of the needs of the national economy and because private companies could not operate or modernise them at a large enough profit.

- Government or state control of industry had also been necessary during the war – so there was **no real opposition from the Conservatives when Labour nationalised the Bank of England (1946), the coal industry (1947), the railways and electricity and gas (1948)**.

- Many socialists and trade unionists were disappointed, because the nationalisations were overseen by **Herbert Morrison**, who did not believe in ideas about workers' self-management.

- Instead, his style of public ownership was merely to establish state ownership, then to leave national boards to manage the industries as they saw fit.

>> practice questions

Study Source A, then answer the question below.

DOTHEBOYS HALL

Source A:
A cartoon from *Punch*, 1948, showing Anuerin Bevan as Mrs Squeers in *Nicholas Nickleby*, giving doctors their NHS medicine

What is the message of this cartoon? Use details of the cartoon and your knowledge to explain.

Politics and society, 1945–79

- During much of the 1950s and 1960s, there were several important social and political issues.

- These concerned immigration and race relations, the situation in Northern Ireland and the emergence of the Swinging Sixties and the student movement.

A Immigration and race relations

>> **key fact** After the Second World War, an increasing number of immigrants arrived from parts of the Commonwealth, such as the West Indies, India and Pakistan and, later, Africa.

- **Labour and Conservative governments actively encouraged this** – to recruit sufficient workers for the new NHS and other expanding public services, such as transport.

- The new immigrants often faced racial discrimination in housing and employment, and even violence. Sometimes, the violence was large-scale – **in 1958, there were race riots in Nottingham and Notting Hill, London**.

- This led to a **series of acts dealing with immigration, racial discrimination and race relations**: 1962 Commonwealth Immigration Act (Conservative); 1965 Race Relations Act (Labour); 1968 Commonwealth Immigration Act (Labour); 1971 Immigration Act (Conservative); 1976 Race Relations Act (Labour).

- **In 1968, Enoch Powell (Conservative) made his infamous 'Rivers of Blood' speech.** During the late 1960s and the 1970s, far-right political parties such as the National Front (NF) and the British National Party (BNP) tried to gain support by stirring up racial hatred.

remember >>

When Enoch Powell was Conservative Minister of Health, he had toured the West Indies to persuade more people to emigrate to Britain and work in the NHS.

B Northern Ireland

>> **key fact** Since the division of Ireland in 1922 (into Northern Ireland and the southern Republic of Ireland), tensions between Unionists (mostly Protestant) and Republicans (mostly Catholic) had generally faded.

- However, in the 1960s, trouble flared up again over the question of **civil rights for Catholics**.

- For decades, the Protestant majority had **discriminated against Catholics** over jobs and housing – there was even **electoral gerrymandering** of local electoral boundaries.

- **In 1963, reforms were promised by Terence O'Neill**, the newly elected prime minister for Northern Ireland. However, by 1967, little had changed.

- To protest against this, the **Northern Ireland Civil Rights Association (NICRA)** was set up.

- Their protest marches were attacked by violent Protestant mobs – and even the **B Special police**. These 'Troubles' led to the **revival of the IRA**, which at first tried to protect Catholic areas from Protestant rioters.

- As the violence increased, **the British government sent in troops in 1969** and, in 1970, the B Specials were disbanded. However, the protests and the violence continued – in 1971, **internment without trial was introduced**.

- This led to still more protests – during a protest march in Londonderry on **30 January 1972**, British troops opened fire and **thirteen demonstrators were killed in what became known as** 'Bloody Sunday'.

- Following this, **Stormont was replaced by Direct Rule**, and the more militant members of the IRA split away to form the **Provisional IRA**, who then began a widespread campaign of bombing and terrorist attacks on British troops and on the British mainland.

- Attempts at power-sharing during the 1970s – such as in 1974 – failed, and the violence continued.

remember >>

The police force in Northern Ireland (the RUC) was mainly Protestant; the part-time police unit known as the B Specials was entirely Protestant, and many were members of the Orange Order.

C Youth culture and student protests

>> **key fact** After the Second World War, life in Britain was still hard at first – rationing of some products continued into the 1950s.

- However, as the 1950s continued, **increasing prosperity** meant many young people had money to spend on clothes, records and films.

- From the mid-1950s, they were influenced by skiffle and rock 'n' roll – and various subcultures emerged (e.g. the Teddy Boys and the Beatniks).

- The 1960s saw the emergence of the Beatles and the 'Liverpool Sound' and the Rolling Stones. Youth subcultures in the 1960s included the mods and rockers and the hippy movement; in the 1970s, the punks emerged.

- Many young people also took an interest in politics. The first big political movement to attract strong youth interest was the **CND campaign in the 1950s and early 1960s** against nuclear weapons.

- As the 1960s progressed, issues such as **apartheid in South Africa, women's liberation and the USA's war in Vietnam** led to protests. In the 1970s came involvement in the **Anti-Nazi League** and **Rock Against Racism** – to counter the violent racist activities of far-right groups such as the National Front and the British National Party.

- There was also greater activity by the **Women's Liberation Movement** in its campaigns on issues such as equal pay, discrimination, domestic violence and the portrayal of women as sex objects by the media.

>> practice questions

1 In what year did race riots break out in Nottingham and Notting Hill, London?

2 What organisation was set up by Catholics who were angry about the discrimination and inequalities they faced in Northern Ireland?

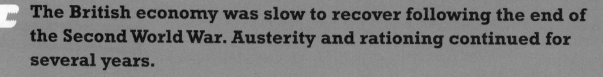

Britain's economy – boom and bust

- ✴ The British economy was slow to recover following the end of the Second World War. Austerity and rationing continued for several years.

- ✴ Although the situation improved in the late 1950s, the underlying trend was long-term economic decline.

- ✴ These economic problems led to several conflicts in industrial relations between employers and trade unions.

A Consumerism

>> **key fact** On the surface, Britain seemed increasingly affluent from the mid-1950s onwards, prompting Tory prime minister Harold MacMillan to say, 'You've never had it so good.'

- One indication of increased prosperity was the **expansion of household consumer goods**, such as vacuum cleaners, fridges and washing machines.

- Another sign was the rapid expansion of **car ownership** – no longer the preserve of the wealthy minority.

- Another significant development was the great increase in the number of families having **televisions** and, later, **telephones**.

remember >>

The 1960s also saw the start of cheap package holidays abroad, made possible by the massive development of air travel.

B Government intervention

>> **key fact** During the Conservatives' thirteen years of power, from 1951 to 1964, Britain's balance of payments deficit increased as Britain's share of world trade fell and imports exceeded exports. This showed how other countries – such as the USA, West Germany and Japan – were benefiting from having modernised their industries.

- These developments led to problems of **inflation** in Britain from the 1950s to the 1970s. The main problems, however, were **the slowness of British companies to invest their profits in newer technologies**, Britain's reliance on the banking and finance sectors to make up for the **growing trade deficit** and the reluctance of some trade unions to change **work practices**, if these led to unemployment.

- The Labour government of 1945–51 had appealed for voluntary wage restraint to help the economy and the Tories, from 1951 to 1964, had at first continued such calls, setting up a **National Incomes Commission in 1962**. The trade unions opposed this, as real wages were being eroded by price inflation.

- The new Labour government of 1964–70 tried to modernise the British economy, although the old problems of industrial decline and inflation continued.

- In 1964, the new Labour government set up a National Board for Prices and Incomes, which mainly tried to control wages.

remember >>

In 1967, Britain's economic problems led to the devaluation of the pound.

C Industrial relations

>> key fact The main way in which governments – both Tory and Labour – dealt with Britain's economic decline was to increasingly intervene in pay settlements and to limit trade union rights to call strikes. A particular problem was the ability of local shop stewards and trade unionists to call unofficial, or 'wildcat', strikes.

- Increasingly, **pay rises were linked to increased productivity**. Such measures continued from the late 1960s into the 1970s, under both the Conservatives (1970–4) and Labour (1974–9).

- As the inflation rate rose, **strikes against falling real wages and rising unemployment became more common** – especially in the public sector (such as the nationalised rail and mining industries and local government), where governments were more able to impose **wage controls and even wage freezes**.

- Consequently, governments increasingly tried to **reform industrial relations** and, especially, to limit trade union rights to call and conduct strikes by introducing new laws – in **1967**, Labour tried unsuccessfully with its **In place of strife** policy, while the Conservatives brought in the **Industrial Relations Act 1972**.

- Such attempts resulted in several bitter strikes – some of which had an increasingly political dimension.

remember >>

Strikes by the miners in 1972 and 1974 were seen as playing a part in the defeat of Edward Heath's 1970–4 Conservative government in the February 1974 election.

>> practice questions

Study Sources A and B below, then answer the question below.

Source A: Workers at a small firm called Grunswick in London picketing in June 1977 over the bussing in of non-union strike-breakers during a dispute over the right to belong to a trade union

Source B: Cartoon published in the *Observer*, April 1979, suggesting trade union power had brought down two prime ministers (Heath and Callaghan) in the years 1974–9. The *Observer* was not as anti-union as many other newspapers at that time.

Which source do you think gives a more accurate view of the state of industrial relations in Britain in the period 1970–9? Use the details of the sources and your own knowledge to explain your answer.

Britain and the world

 As Britain's economy steadily declined in the three decades following the Second World War, so did Britain's position as a world power.

Loss of empire saw Britain decline from being a first-rank power. Increasingly, the post-1945 world was dominated by the USA – a global superpower – and the USSR, which was a regional superpower in Europe.

These developments led to changing relationships with the rest of Europe and the USA.

A End of empire

>> key fact The first significant sign of Britain's decline as a world power came very soon after the end of the Second World War.

- **In 1947**, decades of struggle for national independence by Indian nationalists such as Gandhi and Jinnah saw Britain's Labour government finally accept **Indian independence**, although India was then partitioned into India and Pakistan.

- **In 1948, Britain handed its mandate over Palestine** to the new United Nations, after an increasingly bloody terrorist campaign by Zionist paramilitary groups.

- In the late 1950s and early 1960s, increasing nationalist resistance in African colonies, such as Kenya, led to **wide-scale decolonisation** under Conservative governments – **in 1960, MacMillan made his famous 'Winds of change' speech**.

- An attempt by a Conservative government, led by prime minister **Anthony Eden**, to reassert British power abroad in a dispute with the Egyptian leader, Nasser, led to the **Suez fiasco of 1956**. The secret plot between Britain, France and Israel to invade Egypt led to strong condemnation by the USA.

- Britain also fought nationalist movements in Malaya and Cyprus.

> **remember >>**
>
> At its height, Britain's empire took 30 per cent of British exports and 25 per cent of its investment.

B The European Union

>> key fact The loss of empire – and its economic benefits – increasingly exposed Britain's declining economy.

- One response was to develop the **Commonwealth** to maintain trade links. Its unity was tested by crises resulting from racist governments in South Africa in 1961 and Rhodesia (now called Zimbabwe) in 1965.

- Another response in **1960** was an attempt to join the **European Coal and Steel Community (ECSC)**, which was set up in 1951 – from 1 January 1958, following the signing of a new treaty in 1957, this became the **EEC**.

> **remember >>**
>
> The six members of the EEC were France, West Germany, Italy and the three Benelux countries.

- At first, British governments preferred being linked to the USA and the Commonwealth. However, although both Conservative and Labour governments tried to join in the 1960s, these attempts were unsuccessful. This was mainly because of **French objections to Britain's subservience to the USA**.

- In 1970, the new Conservative government under Heath tried again – this time the application was successful, and **Britain became a member in 1973**. However, despite calls for a referendum on the issue, none was held.

- **In 1975, the newly elected Labour government under Harold Wilson** honoured its election promise to hold a referendum on continued membership of the EEC – the electorate voted two to one to stay in.

remember >>

Although Britain remained a member of the EEC after 1975, the debate as to the wisdom of membership continued throughout the decade.

C The 'special relationship'

>> key fact As Britain's power in the world declined, greater emphasis was placed by successive British governments on the 'special relationship' with the USA.

- As the Cold War developed, and Britain's economy declined, **Britain became increasingly dependent on the USA**. In order to join and stay in the 'nuclear club', Britain had to rely on the USA for nuclear warheads – **in 1960**, Britain's **Blue Streak missile was abandoned in favour of the USA's Skybolt** and, later, its **Polaris**.

- Signs of this 'special relationship' were the increasing number of **US military bases on British territory** (beyond those established during the Second World War) and the willingness of British governments to help the USA in the wider world by maintaining a **British military presence 'East of Suez'**, even though the economy could not afford it.

- The defence costs of playing this supporting role for US foreign policy was one of the main reasons for Britain's growing economic problems. Eventually, despite US objections, **Britain was forced to abandon its military outposts**.

remember >>

Although British governments did not send troops to help the USA in Vietnam, they did give support and encouraged Commonwealth countries such as Australia to send troops there.

>> practice questions

1 Harold MacMillan's 'Winds of change' speech was concerned with which developments in Africa?

2 In what year did the Conservative prime minister Edward Heath take Britain into the EEC?

Women in the 1950s

 Women had played an important role in the Second World War – in the armed forces and on the home front.

 After the Second World War, the task of rebuilding Britain needed a massive labour force – governments used women as part of this, unlike at the end of the First World War, when women were forced out of jobs.

 Women also benefited from the new social welfare reforms that were introduced after 1945. However, the question of equality soon emerged.

A Impact of the Second World War

>> key fact Reconstruction after the Second World War required a massive labour force – the returning ex-servicemen were not enough. As well as recruiting additional labour from Commonwealth countries, governments in the 1950s encouraged women to stay at work.

- Older married women responded, while younger married women with young children were less keen – **many still saw the main role of women as housewife/mother**. Women's magazines continued to focus on these traditional roles.

- **To get more women to work**, governments encouraged employers to provide laundries at work, offer part-time and shift work and arrange for shops to deliver household goods to factories. Schools were asked to remain open longer and during the holidays.

remember >>

Despite these initiatives, it was difficult to encourage women to work in textiles, where they experienced particularly low pay and poor conditions. These jobs were later filled by new immigrants from Commonwealth countries.

B Social welfare reforms

>> key fact To help keep women in the workforce, governments also allocated resources to build nurseries.

- **Women especially benefited from the establishment of the Welfare State and the National Health Service**, which were set up by the 1945–51 Labour government and placed great emphasis on the needs of women, especially as regards childbirth, child care and contraception.

- One result of these changes was that, proportionately, **women spent a smaller part of their lives child-bearing and nursing young** – this did much to improve women's health.

- Consequently, women's life expectancy increased in the second half of the twentieth century, **allowing many more women to begin, or resume, careers after their children reached school age.**

remember >>

The contraceptive pill became available during the 1950s.

>> **key fact** Although it was more common for married women to work, it was mostly only in certain areas that they found employment. Also, in some respects, little had changed – in particular, women were still paid, on average, half of what men earned.

- One problem was the **question of promotion**. Most women were in part-time employment, in order to fit in with what most people saw as their primary housewife/mother role.

- **The same inequalities existed in relation to wages and salaries**, with most women in the 1950s working in low-paid employment as secretaries and factory or shop workers. It was **rare for women to occupy important professional jobs** in areas such as law, medicine, journalism, the civil service or the finance sector – yet it was here that the higher salaries were to be found.

- There were women who managed to achieve success in such professions – **they were very much the exception, not the rule**.

remember >>

In 1948, seven million women were in some kind of paid employment; by 1957, 29 per cent of married women were in the workforce.

remember >>

The inequalities experienced by women were linked to education in schools, where subjects such as domestic science were taught only to girls.

>> practice questions

1 How did the NHS and the new Welfare State, set up under Labour from 1945–51, affect the ability of women to have paid employment outside the home?

2 What secondary school subject was taught only to girls in the 1950s?

Women's liberation in the 1960s

- During the 1960s, the inequalities affecting women became increasingly apparent and objectionable to many women.

- At the same time, the extension of electricity and new domestic technology meant women were increasingly released from some of the back-breaking household chores.

- This extra time allowed more women to pursue careers – and to reflect on sexist male attitudes that predominated in society.

A The new feminism

>> **key fact** By the 1960s, many women felt little progress had been made towards equality for women.

- One area was **education** – although girls did well in GCE O-level exams, relatively few stayed on to take A-levels in the sixth form. Consequently, men outnumbered women at university by three to one.

- Also, because of prevailing attitudes to the traditional housewife/ mother role of women, girls often took subjects such as cookery and textiles and were **not encouraged to go into the sciences**.

B Impact of new technologies

>> **key fact** New technologies after the Second World War greatly improved the lives of many women – especially when electricity, gas and water companies connected supplies to more and more houses during the 1950s and 1960s.

- Access to electricity meant women could have **labour-saving domestic appliances** such as refrigerators, freezers, vacuum cleaners and washing machines.

- All these **greatly reduced the amount of time spent on household chores** such as shopping, cleaning the house and washing clothes.

- This 'saved' time meant more women were able to work and so became more aware of the inequalities in the workplace as regards wages and promotion prospects – the so-called **glass ceiling**.

- In addition, it meant women had more time to reflect on **feminist arguments** about these issues, and the general sexist attitudes to women that existed in society as a whole.

C Campaign issues

From the late 1960s, a women's liberation movement began to emerge. Local groups were set up all over the country.

- Inspired by feminist writers such as **Germaine Greer** and her 1969 book *The Female Eunuch*, they began to hold **'consciousness-raising' meetings** to discuss such issues as male attitudes to women and discrimination at work. By 1969, most major British towns had a Women's Liberation group.

- Partly as a result of their campaigns, the Labour government of 1964–70 passed several reforms:

remember >>

Extra publicity was gained at 'bra-burning' events, when, in the late 1960s, some women showed their objections to stereotypical male-dominated ideas about how women were supposed to look and dress.

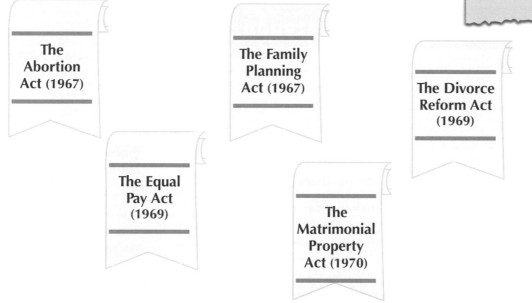

The Abortion Act (1967)

The Family Planning Act (1967)

The Divorce Reform Act (1969)

The Equal Pay Act (1969)

The Matrimonial Property Act (1970)

>> practice questions

Study Source A, then briefly explain the key demands of feminists in Britain in the 1960s.

> The first exercise of the free woman is to devise her mode [method] of revolt, which will reflect her own independence and originality. If women are the true proletariat [working class], the oppressed majority, the revolution can only be drawn nearer by their withdrawal of support for the capitalist system.

Source A: An extract from Germaine Greer's book, *The Female Eunuch*, 1969

Equality in the 1970s?

 The development of the Women's Liberation Movement saw a growing variety of campaigns against the various issues affecting women.

 The protests, and the growth of feminist magazines, put increasing pressure on governments to pass more reforms to address these issues.

 However, despite various gains in the 1970s, several issues continued to show that women still experienced inequality and male dominance.

A An agenda for women's liberation

>> **key fact** In 1970, the various local Women's Liberation groups met at a National Conference, and agreed on four main demands:
- equal pay
- equal education and opportunity
- 24-hour nurseries
- free contraception and abortion on demand.

- Feminist magazines and journals – such as *Spare Rib* and *Shrew* – were set up. These, and the many marches and demonstrations, helped to publicise the cause of women's liberation and the need to reject male-dominated views about what defines female 'beauty'.

- As well as equality in education and at work, the Women's Liberation Movement also **opposed male sexist and chauvinist attitudes** to women – especially the idea that the housework and childcare roles could only be done by women.

remember >>

Feminists also set up a publishing company, Virago, to help spread feminist writings and ideas.

B Reforms of the 1970s

>> **key fact** Other important reforms were passed in the 1970s, mainly by the Labour government of 1974–9:

remember >>

The paid leave after childbirth under the 1975 Act was at 90 per cent of earnings.

Sex Discrimination Act 1975
Made discrimination on the grounds of gender illegal

Domestic Violence Act 1977
Gave some protection for women against violent husbands

Equality reforms of the 70s

Employment Protection Act 1975
Gave mothers employed for two years the right to return to their former employment – although not the same job – within 29 weeks of giving birth; plus 18 weeks' paid leave, if they returned to full-time work

C Continuing problems

>> **key fact** Despite these important reforms, it often proved difficult to enforce the laws – many employers, and, at first, some of the male-dominated trade unions, were opposed.

- Sexual harrassment at work was a new issue that had emerged by the late 1970s – and one that continues to be difficult to prove. The glass ceiling issue also continued to cause problems.

- Traditional attitudes about what was 'proper' for a woman continued to persist. Even the **Employment Protection Act 1975**, by only giving paid leave to women, seemed to accept that the childcare role was not one that fathers would wish to share.

- In addition to issues of employment and politics, women were increasingly angered by the growing **sexualisation of women in the media** – and by what was seen as a resulting increase in sexual harrassment and **violence against women on the streets and in the home**.

- In particular, the Women's Liberation Movement began to give more prominence to the issue of **domestic violence**.

- **In 1971, Erin Pizzey was the first person to set up a refuge** for women and their children escaping from violent partners – inspired by her example, many more refuges began to appear.

remember >>

Typical of the growing media portrayal of women as sex objects was Rupert Murdoch's tabloid newspaper, *The Sun*, which, in 1970, became the first national daily newspaper to feature a photograph of a topless woman.

>> practice questions

Study Sources A and B, then answer the question below.

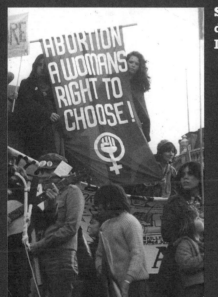

Source A: 1970s abortion demonstration, showing the Women's Liberation symbol on the banner

Source B: A Women's Liberation demonstration, protesting about the way in which marriage restricts women

Which source is more useful in telling you about the concerns of the Women's Liberation Movement in Britain in the 1970s? Use details from the sources and your knowledge to explain your answer.

Exam questions and model answers

>> Sections 1 and 2: Comprehension in context/ recall

Study Sources A and B below, which refer to the early stages of the First World War, and then answer the question that follows.

Source A Map of the aims of the Schlieffen Plan before 1914

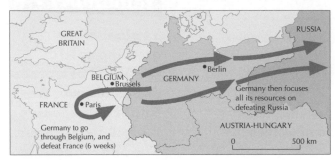

Source B Extract from a history textbook, published in 1996

> The war became a stalemate because the techniques and weapons were better suited to defence than to attack. It was much easier to defend a position than to attack one. The machine gun could mow down charging soldiers. Barbed wire, trenches and mud made cavalry charges ineffective.

>> Question

Explain, briefly, what you understand by the terms:

(a) 'Schlieffen Plan' in Source A

(b) 'stalemate' in Source B. **4 marks**

>> Answering this type of question

A   What skills do I need?

You are expected to:

1   **give a clear definition** of any term(s) mentioned in the question

2   **extract information** from the source(s) and/ or from the details about the source provided by the Principal Examiner

3   **comment on any impression** the writer of a source is trying to create

4   remember to **use your own knowledge** to explain any terms and what is in the source.

B   Extra tips

In order to do well in exams, you need to do more than the minimum.

So follow these steps:

1   **Give some precise information** from the source itself (such as names) and/or from the attribution/ provenance details.

2   Remember to **add a few exact, new factual details from your own knowledge** to explain terms in the source(s) and **add extra information** to explain what is being referred to/what perspective is being shown.

C   Remember

*   **Make sure you read through your answer at some point to check that you have made specific references to the source(s) AND used your own knowledge.**

*   Such questions usually carry relatively low marks, so don't write half a page or more. Normally, a couple of sentences, with a few precise, relevant comments and facts will be sufficient to obtain full marks.

>> Model answer

(a) The Schlieffen Plan was the **German war plan**. It was based on the belief that in a war involving France and Russia against Germany, *France could be defeated before the Russian army could be mobilised, so avoiding a two-front war.* But this did not happen because *the Russians mobilised before the outbreak of war.*

(b) Stalemate means that **neither side was able to break through and defeat the other.** This was because, **as shown in Source B, the weapons were better for defence.** The stalemate came about *after the race to the sea and the building of a network of trenches.*

Why this answer scores full marks

*   The parts in bold give brief and accurate explanations of the two terms. On their own, these would get the candidate half marks. In (b), there is also a specific reference to the relevant source.

*   The parts in italics add extra information from the candidate's own knowledge – these gain the extra two marks.

>> Section 3: Recall/key features

>> Question

Describe the key features of the show trials in the Soviet Union during the 1930s. **6 marks**

Answering this type of question

A   What skills do I need?

You are expected to:

1   **give a clear explanation/show an overall grasp** of the aspect you have been asked to describe

2   use your own knowledge to **provide a detailed description with precise supporting facts**

3   try to **give a wider view/the overall context**.

B   Remember

Look carefully at the marks available. Don't write half a page or more if the question only carries two or three marks. If it carries five or six marks, write a couple of paragraphs.

>> Model answer

The show trials were open or public trials in the years 1936–8, in which leading Communists who opposed Stalin were arrested. They were then put on trial for offences they had not committed (such as sabotage, plotting against Stalin or being secret agents for capitalist countries). They were forced to admit to these 'crimes' in these public show trials. This was done by sleep deprivation, beatings and threats to their families. The evidence was usually false and they had no proper chance to defend themselves. They were then found 'guilty' and many were imprisoned or even executed. This was done to stop any Communist leaders from daring to oppose Stalin. Later, even engineers were accused in what became known as the Great Purge and Terror. This frightened people and helped to keep Stalin as dictator of the Communist Party and the USSR.

Why this answer scores full marks

- The answer shows **clear understanding of the trials** (the victims, what happened during the trials, the types of punishment).

- There is **detailed supporting information** (dates, 'crimes').

- There is a **developed explanation of their purpose** (to keep Stalin in power).

>> Section 4: Utility/accuracy/ reliability/questions

Source A An extract from a book written in 1940 by a former Nazi who left Germany in 1934. He is reporting a conversation he had in 1934 with a drunken Ernst Rohm, leader of the SA.

Adolf is a swine. He is betraying all of us now. He is becoming friendly with army generals . . . We are revolutionaries, aren't we? The generals are a lot of old stick-in-the-muds. I am the centre of the new army, don't they see that?

>> Question

How useful is this source as evidence of the threat the SA posed to Hitler in 1934? **6 marks**

Answering this type of question

A   What skills do I need?

You are expected to:

1   **comment on the content/information** given by the source(s)

2   **use the provenance/attribution information** provided, to **comment on the limitations/ typicality/purpose** of the source(s).

B   Remember

- If the question asks you to decide which of two (or more) sources is the most reliable/ useful, you must **comment on ALL the sources AND make a choice**.

- If it is a utility question, make sure you mention the words **useful** or **uses** in your answer.

>> Model answer

Source A is useful to an extent because it shows that Rohm, the SA leader, was very angry in 1934 – he wanted to be the head of a new German army, he hated the present generals and he believed Hitler was betraying the Nazi Party. This was a threat to Hitler as the SA had about two million members by 1934.

However, this source has reliability problems. It was written in 1940, six years after the conversation took place, and after the Night of the Long Knives. Maybe the writer didn't remember accurately what Rohm said, or he might be trying to justify Hitler's actions.

Also, Rohm was drunk so might not have meant all he said; and Hitler was very popular with many in the SA – so not all of them would have supported Rohm.

Why this answer scores full marks

- **It deals with the content** (reasons why Rohm is angry).
- **It uses the provenance information** given in the caption (author, dates, the fact that Rohm was drunk).
- **It is balanced**, showing **limitations** as well as uses, and comments on possible purpose.

>> Section 5: Cross-referencing questions

Study Sources A, B and C below, which refer to Roosevelt and the New Deal, and then answer the question that follows.

Source A From a history textbook written in 1991

> In 1935 the Supreme Court said the National Industrial Recovery Act was illegal. In 1936, the same thing happened to the Agricultural Adjustment Act. To Roosevelt it seemed wrong that the Supreme Court, which was not elected by the people, should be able to stop the introduction of laws that both he and Congress thought the nation needed. To get round this opposition, Roosevelt planned to appoint additional judges to the Court.

Source B From a political speech by Herbert Hoover, 1937

> Freedom is crumbling in over two-thirds of the world. The people's security in those countries has gone out of the window. And – in every instance – those in power have said they were acting for their people in the name of progress. Every American has cause to be anxious for our country. We have already gone far on the road to personal government. The American people must halt these changes to the independence of the Supreme Court.

Source C From an article in a US newspaper written in 1937

> If the American people accept the President's changes to the Supreme Court without letting out a yell to high heaven, they will no longer be protecting their liberties. This is the beginning of pure, personal government. The President is already powerful. If the Supreme Court is to have a majority chosen by the President, we will have a one-man government.

>> Question

Does Source C support the evidence of Sources A and B about Roosevelt's difficulties with the Supreme Court? **4 marks**

Answering this type of question

A   What skills do I need?

You are expected to:

1   **make clear/precise references** to ALL the sources mentioned – they don't have to be long

2   **show how the sources are similar AND how they differ** (e.g. extra facts, different figures).

B   Remember

- Describing/copying out/rephrasing what the sources say/show **is NOT comparing them**.

- Once you've shown how the sources are similar, write a sentence beginning, 'However, although Source C says . . . this is not supported by Source A, which . . . '

>> Model answer

Source C describes Roosevelt's attempts to alter the membership of the Supreme Court, and warns that he could be setting up 'personal' or 'one-man government'. To an extent, this supports Source A as it says he wanted to appoint 'additional judges' to the Court. However, Source A differs from Source C, as it says Roosevelt and Congress – not just Roosevelt himself – only wanted the changes to help give 'the nation' what it 'needed'. This was to pass New Deal reforms, which had been blocked by the unelected Court – so he can't have been as 'powerful' as Source C says. Source C also doesn't say anything about those difficulties, which is why Roosevelt wanted to change the judges – it just tries to make him out as a would-be dictator.

Source C supports Source B much more. They both mention the dangers of 'personal government'. Source C is probably from a newspaper that supported the Republicans, which is why it agrees so much with Source B, which is a speech by Hoover, who was the

Republican president defeated by Roosevelt in 1932. These two both make Roosevelt out to be a dictator. Both Sources C and B fail to mention Roosevelt's problems with the Supreme Court.

Why this answer scores full marks

- There are **clear and supported** C–A and C–B cross-references (Supreme Court judges, personal rule).

- As well as showing agreement, there is also an example of **how the sources differ**, linked to the issue of Roosevelt's difficulties with the Supreme Court.

>> Section 6: Source-sufficiency questions

Study Sources A and B below, which are about Germany's invasion of the USSR during the Second World War, and then answer the question that follows.

Source A Extract from a radio speech by Stalin, 3 July 1941

> In case of a forced retreat of Red Army units, all [railway] stock must be evacuated, the enemy must not be left a single engine, a single railway truck … Collective farmers must drive off all their cattle and turn over their grain to the safe keeping of the State authorities … All valuable property that cannot be withdrawn must be destroyed without fail …

Source B Soviet partisan fighters in 1942

>> Question

Do Sources A and B provide enough information to explain why Nazi Germany's Operation Barbarossa eventually failed? Use the sources, and your own knowledge, to explain your answer. **8 marks**

Answering this type of question

A What skills do I need?

You are expected to:

1 **make use of all the sources** given, commenting on content AND any reliability problems

2 **give precise information/'other factors' from your own knowledge,** not contained in the sources.

B Remember

Use the sources **AND** your own knowledge – if you only do one of these things, you will only get half marks at most.

>> Model answer

These sources only provide some of the reasons why the Germans lost the war on the Eastern Front. Source A (although it is a radio speech by Stalin and so might be propaganda) refers to scorched earth policy, which left the Germans without food or shelter as they advanced into the USSR. Source B shows Soviet partisans, who disrupted German supply lines.

Although these are both reasons why Nazi Germany lost, there were other factors. These include the severe Russian winter, which the Germans were not prepared for – the invasion in June 1941 was later than originally planned. Also, Hitler interfered too much with military decisions, while Stalin left tactics to the Red Army commanders. Also important were the Five-Year Plans, and the decision to move equipment behind the Ural Mountains – this meant that the USSR massively outproduced Germany in arms production, such as tanks and planes.

Why this answer scores full marks

- **BOTH** the sources are used, and shown to be important reasons.

- The candidate's own knowledge is then used to provide a range of 'other factors'.

>> Section 7: Recall/causation/explanation questions

>> Question

Explain why the Warsaw Pact formed in 1955.
6 marks

Answering this type of question

A What skills do I need?

You are expected to:

1 **give a range of different reasons/ explanations**

2 **use your own detailed knowledge** to support each of the explanations given.

B Remember

- With 'why' (or 'how') questions, you need to explain why something happened – not just describe what happened.

- Don't be satisfied with just one reason – try to give several different reasons.

- You must do more than just give a list of different reasons – so give detailed/precise supporting facts.

>> Model answer

There were several reasons why the USSR set up the Warsaw Pact in 1955. The short-term reason was the West's decision to rearm West Germany and allow it to join NATO. But the long-term reasons were Soviet fears of the USA, and the division of Germany.

Since 1945, the USSR had feared that a Germany rebuilt by US Marshall Aid might be a threat in the future. As the Cold War developed, these fears increased – especially as the USA had a nuclear weapons monopoly until 1949. When the West united their zones of Germany into 'Trizonia' and introduced a new currency in 1948, without consulting the USSR, Stalin began the Berlin Blockade
to force the West out of West Berlin, which was in the Soviet zone of Eastern Germany.

But this failed and instead led to the formation of NATO and West Germany in 1949. This only increased Soviet fears as, at that time, the USSR had no military alliance of its own. Although the USSR exploded its first nuclear bomb in 1949, the USA still had superiority. Then the USA set up other alliances, such as SEATO in 1953 and the Baghdad Pact in 1954.

Because the USSR saw the Eastern European countries as its 'buffer zone', it finally set up its own alliance in 1955 – the Warsaw Pact – which was to include all those countries. So, the Warsaw Pact was the USSR's response to NATO and West Germany being allowed to join it – but it was much weaker than NATO.

Why this answer scores full marks

- There are several different explanations given, which are even separated into short- and long-term reasons.

- The answer is well organised – so a rough plan has probably been worked out.

- There is also plenty of precise, supporting information (dates, events).

>> Section 8: Source evaluation questions

Source A This photograph shows 15-year-old Elizabeth Eckford on her way to the previously all-white Central High School in Little Rock, Arkansas, in September 1957. She is surrounded by a hostile mob of white students and adults.

>> Question

Study Source A. Why was this photograph published so widely in the USA?

Use details from the photograph and your own knowledge to explain your answer. **8 marks**

Answering this type of question

A   What skills do I need?

You are expected to:

1   **comment on and interpret the content/ information** given by the source and **add your own knowledge to explain its context**

2   **explain what message** is being presented by the source

3   **explain the purpose** of the source and its message.

B   Remember

- Just describing what the source shows will **NOT** get you high marks.

- Do not forget to use precise details from your own knowledge to explain your answer.

>> Model answer

This photograph shows Elizabeth Eckford being escorted and protected by US paratroopers, who had been sent by President Eisenhower to uphold the Supreme Court ruling that racial segregation in public schools was illegal. Eisenhower had done this when Governor Faubus of Arkansas, as part of his opposition to the desegregation of schools, refused to protect the black students.

The women and students are clearly angry – one woman is screaming at her. The message of this photograph is that there is a lot of white racism and anti-black feeling in this Southern state, and that it is so bad that the US president believes troops are needed to protect the small number of black students wanting to go to school.

The reason for publishing this photograph throughout the USA was probably to show the problems faced by black students and to get more support for the Civil Rights Movement's campaign for desegregation, by showing Americans how violently opposed many whites were to desegregation.
By showing how calm and dignified the girl is, despite being shouted and spat at, the purpose of this photograph might also be to put the opponents of desegregation in a bad light.

Why this answer scores full marks

- As well as **comments on relevant aspects of the content** of the source, there are explicit attempts to **explain the MESSAGE of the source – AND** to clearly **identify a possible PURPOSE**.

- There are also **several precise pieces of own knowledge to explain the historical context of the source** (Supreme Court ruling against segregation in education, events in Little Rock, actions of the Governor of Arkansas and President Eisenhower).

>> Sections 9 –13: Recall/ judgement questions

Study Sources A, B and C below, which are about the role played by women in Britain during the Second World War, and then answer the question that follows.

Source A Government recruitment poster for women munitions workers

Source B Table showing the number of women involved in uniformed services

Auxiliary Territorial Service	198 000
Women's Land Army	30 000
Civil Defence	375 000
Armed forces	470 000

Source C Members of the Women's Land Army at work, 1942

>> Question

'The contribution made by women in Britain during the Second World War was restricted to helping with war production.' Do you agree with this statement?

Use the sources, and your own knowledge, to explain your answer. **10 marks**

Answering this type of question

A What skills do I need?

You are expected to:

1 **use most of the sources** mentioned (if there are five or six, it isn't necessary to use all of them)

2 **add plenty of precise own knowledge** to add to what the sources give, and to mention aspects they don't

3 **produce a balanced answer** that looks at both sides **AND** provides a **range of issues/factors**.

B Remember

- You will only get half marks if you deal only with sources or your own knowledge – you must do **BOTH** to score high marks.

- Make sure your facts are detailed – don't give general/vague references.

>> Model answer

I think this statement is only partly correct, as British women were involved in lots of other areas that were not connected to war production. It is true, as Sources A and C show, that many did do production work – either in munitions factories (as they did in the First World War) as Source A shows, or farm work, which is shown in Sources B and C. Women helped replace men who had been conscripted. In fact, in 1941, all single women aged 19–30 were conscripted into essential war work or the women's armed forces.

However, none of the sources show the other work done by women, such as making uniforms, boots and medical supplies. Also, many women drove lorries, buses and trams or worked on the railways. Other jobs done by women included office work, such as the civil service; working for the post office sorting and delivering letters; and work with various voluntary organisations such as the WVS.

As well as war work, many women acted as nurses in the FANY, which had been set up in the previous war. Women were also involved in the women's sections of the armed forces – Source B says 470 000; these were the WRNS, the WRAF and the WRAC. Also, as Source B shows, women joined the ATS (with some working on the anti-aircraft batteries, even during the worst of the Blitz) and the Civil Defence (about 100 000 acted as ARP wardens to help with air raids). None of the sources mentions the ATA – some of the women in the ATA flew newly produced planes from the factories to their air bases.

Finally, although women in the armed forces already mentioned were not allowed to take part in combat, some women agents of the SOE were – mainly in Nazi-occupied France, with twelve being shot by the Germans. So, overall, I disagree with the statement, as women did more than just production work.

Why this answer scores full marks

- It is a **BALANCED** answer, showing both agreement and disagreement with the statement.

- There are clear references to all three sources.

- There is also plenty of precise own knowledge to support the points being made.

Answers to practice questions

Section 1: THE FIRST WORLD WAR, 1890–1918

Long-term causes

1898: Kaiser Wilhelm II decided that Germany should have a big navy.

1906: Britain built the first dreadnought battleship; Germany followed suit.

1913: Germany built Kiel Canal, giving quick access to the North Sea.

Short-term causes

In 1908, Austria–Hungary had annexed Bosnia–Herzegovina, angering the Serb nationalists who lived there, as they wanted to be part of Serbia; in 1914, Franz Ferdinand decided to visit Sarajevo, the capital of Bosnia, giving the Black Hand terrorist group their opportunity.

The war begins

1 Britain declared war because Germany invaded Belgium and refused to withdraw/Britain had signed a treaty to guarantee Belgian independence and neutrality.

2 The main weapons (machine guns, heavy artillery) were more defensive than offensive.

Warfare

1 It reduced British food supplies so much that rationing had to be introduced/Britain almost ran out of food supplies because so many supply ships were sunk.

2 Use of convoy system/zigzag sailing patterns/hydrophones.

The end of the war

1 Source A shows the death rates for civilians in Germany getting significantly worse in the years 1915–18 so that, by 1918, the death rate had risen by more than 300 per cent – from about 90 000 in 1915 to 300 000 in 1918. This could tie in with the fact that the Allied naval blockade of German ports began to cause serious food shortages from 1916 onwards. Source B supports Source A in that it shows German civilians in Berlin scavenging for food in what looks like a rubbish heap – these people must have been very hungry to do this, and this could be the result of the blockade. However, Source A doesn't say that the increased death rate was due to lack of food, so Source B doesn't necessarily support Source A.

2 Source B is useful as it is a photograph taken at the end of 1918, showing that some people in Berlin were so desperate for food that they scavenged in rubbish heaps for scraps. This would be good evidence of how the Allied naval blockade caused food shortages. However, this is only one photograph of one part of one German city – it might not be typical of the rest of Germany (for example, people in rural areas might have been able to grow extra food).

The difficulties of peace-making

1 Britain, France and the USA

2 He thought this because they had borrowed so much money from the USA to pay for the war (war debts)/had also lost so much trade to the USA during the war years/the USA was the world's wealthiest and most powerful country.

3 As President, Wilson was the head of the US government, so would be in a position to know and make government policy. Also, this was a private note, not intended for publication, so he would have no reason to lie. So, overall, it is quite reliable and can be trusted.

The Treaty of Versailles

Source A shows the 'Big Three' (Britain, the USA and France) leaving the Conference Hall in Versailles after the signing of the Treaty of Versailles in June 1919. The cartoonist is saying that the treaty will cause a new war in 1940 because the terms are so harsh on Germany – Clemenceau ('The Tiger') is saying he hears a child ('the 1940 class') weeping. The cartoonist was only one year out, as the Second World War began in 1939. This cartoon from 1919 agrees with the views of J. M. Keynes (a British economist) who also believed the terms were too harsh. This is backed up by Source B, which, ten years later, refers to one of the biggest grievances the Germans felt – reparations (compensation), which they had to pay after being forced to sign the 'War Guilt Clause' (Article 231). The final figure (£6600 million) was not agreed until 1921. Many Germans also resented the restrictions on their armed forces and the loss of European lands to countries such as Poland and France, and the loss of all their colonies.

Assessing the treaties

Source A is a French poster, probably produced by the French government (although it doesn't say so). It shows that the French saw the Germans as murderers ('assassins') and were afraid that they might attack again (probably to take back the provinces of Alsace and Lorraine, which had been returned to France by the Treaty of Versailles in 1919, the year the poster was produced). The poster also shows some of the massive destruction France suffered during the war – this is what made the French determined to get compensation from Germany and to keep it weak. However, this is only one source – in particular, it does not give details about the other things France wanted – for example, to make the Rhineland into a separate state (in the end they had to be satisfied with it being just a de-militarised zone). There is also nothing about how France only became harsher on Germany when they realised that Britain would not support the idea of the League of Nations having its own army to uphold the treaty, and that the USA would not cancel France's war debts.

Section 2: THE LEAGUE OF NATIONS, 1919–39

Establishment of the League

1 The USA was the world's strongest power, so its membership would have made it easier to keep the terms of the treaty in place. Also, the two other main countries, Britain and France, did not always agree on what to do – for example, on whether the terms should be made less harsh on Germany.

2 Germany and Russia

The League in the 1920s

1 The Corfu incident, when Italy invaded Corfu
2 It was finally settled by the Conference of Ambassadors, which ordered Greece to pay 50 million lire as compensation to Italy.

The League in the 1930s

Source A, a contemporary source, refers to the Lytton Report, the weak response from the League and Japan's armed defiance of the League. However, it doesn't provide detailed information. Also, the cartoonist, who is British, seems to be critical of the League, so he may have exaggerated. Although the source comments on the lack of effective action by the League, it does not give the Japanese view.

Section 3: RUSSIA IN REVOLUTION, 1917–41

The end of tsarist Russia

1 The Tsar thought it might create patriotic feelings and so stop the growing strikes and protests against his rule. He also wanted to get a seaport in the Balkans, and so supported Serbia.
2 This was when, after the March Revolution in 1917, there was shared power between the unelected Provisional Government, which replaced the Tsar, and the Petrograd Soviet, which represented workers, soldiers and peasants. In practice, because of Order No. 1, real power lay with the elected Soviet.

The Bolsheviks win power

1 Leon Trotsky
2 The Reds were united/Reds had control of the centre (railways and factories)/Trotsky built up a large and efficient Red Army/the peasants opposed the Whites as they wanted to keep landlords' lands/many people resented foreign intervention on the side of the Whites.

Economic policies under Lenin

These two sources agree and disagree about the success of the NEP. Source A, a table of production figures, shows that after the NEP was introduced in 1921, grain, coal and steel production, and the numbers of cattle and pigs, increased so that, by 1926, they had almost reached the levels of 1913. In fact, the figure for cattle was 62 million by 1925, which was three million higher than in 1913.

Source B, taken from the memoirs of a Bolshevik published in 1987, doesn't really say anything about the successes, but it does say that after NEP, cafés and restaurants started opening. Before then, they had been down to a small piece of bread per person – so more food must have become available, as shown in Source A. However, Source B doesn't say anything about industrial production. It is also different because it shows there was opposition to Lenin's NEP from Bolsheviks, although most supported him.

From Lenin to Stalin

1 Zinoviev, Kamenev and Stalin

2 Stalin's job involved the appointment of party members to important jobs, and their dismissal, and the acceptance or rejection of people as party members. So he was able to promote his own supporters, control important party meetings and isolate his opponents.

Stalin's revolution

1 Heavy industries include coal-mining, steel, iron, oil and electricity – all the industries necessary to build factories and machinery and so bring about industrialisation and modernisation of industry.
2 Stalin brought in skilled foreign workers/introduced piece-rate working and bonuses and privileges for those who produced more ('Stakhanovites')/ encouraged women and peasants to work in factories/ increased working hours/imposed fines for lateness or absenteeism/sent people to gulags to carry out big construction projects.

The approach of war

1 The crisis over the Sudetenland in Czechoslovakia/the Munich Agreement
2 It allowed the USSR to gain extra time for building up Soviet defences/use Poland as a buffer zone when attacked, so fighting would not be on Soviet soil.

Section 4: GERMANY, 1918–45

Changes in Germany

1 The SPD, Centre Party and the DNVP
2 That the form of PR used led to a large number of small parties in the Reichstag – this meant it was difficult for one party to have an overall majority. So most governments were coalitions, which often found it difficult to agree on policies. This became a serious problem during the Great Depression, with lots of changes of governments.

Weimar Germany, 1919–23

1 Germany had not paid its second reparations instalment – the idea was to take coal and steel in place of the money that was owed.
2 Hyperinflation was when the value of the mark fell so quickly and prices rose so rapidly, that workers had to be paid twice a day. Even a stamp cost millions of marks – this caused great poverty, especially for those on pensions.

Germany before the Depression

1 Hitler's attempted March on Berlin of 1923 had been a failure: he'd been put in prison, the Nazis had been banned and had split into factions. Also, he realised he needed the support of wealthy industrialists and the army.
2 He relaunched the Nazi Party and set up special sections for different social groups (e.g. teachers, students, farmers, small shopkeepers). He also set up the Hitler Youth, and the SS. Finally, he made sure he was in total control of the party by expelling those who disagreed with his plans.

The Nazis come to power

1 Once the Nazi dictatorship had been established,

they wanted him to carry out a 'second revolution', that is, for the SA to become the new German army (with Rohm as leader) and for the more left-wing aspects of the Party Programme to be implemented.

2   Shortly after the SS had murdered Rohm and other SA leaders, Hindenburg died. The army generals then supported Hitler taking over the role of President and Commander-in-Chief of the armed forces, as well as remaining Chancellor – he thus became the Führer of Germany. Later, the army swore an oath of loyalty to him.

Maintaining Nazi control

1   As part of the 3 Ks Nazi policy, women were encouraged to stay at home to have babies. To achieve this, they were excluded from state jobs/employers were encouraged to employ only men/loans and medals were given to women who stayed at home and had children. Most of the equal rights women had achieved under the Weimar Republic were removed.

2   Young people were the future generation – they wanted to ensure Nazi support for years to come, and to get Germany ready to fight a war (the girls to increase Germany's population, and the boys to be soldiers).

Outside the Nazi 'community'

1   The source is a photograph taken in 1933 of SA and SS men enforcing the boycott of Jewish shops, which Hitler imposed in April 1933. It is useful in showing what the Nazis tried to do, but it doesn't say the boycott was ended quite quickly because so few non-Jewish Germans followed it. More importantly, it only shows the carrying out of one policy in one year (1933) – there is nothing about other policies in the period 1933–9.

2   These were: laws to sack all Jews from the civil service, the law and education; banning Jewish people from all public places such as parks and swimming pools; the Nuremberg Laws of 1935 (which took away their right to be German citizens, and forbade inter-marriage); Kristallnacht (1938); and making all Jews wear the yellow star of David and add 'Jewish' names to their passports.

Section 5: THE USA, 1919–45

The Republican era begins

It is difficult to decide how far it can be trusted as it doesn't say who took the photograph, or why. Also, it doesn't even say in what year it was taken – it could have been taken in 1929, after the Wall Street Crash. It could have been Democrat propaganda against the Republicans. Even if it is genuine, it might be just an isolated example of one of the poorest states in the USA, and not typical of the whole country in the 1920s before the Depression.

Problems during the boom

1   It gave criminal gangs the opportunity to grow rich/many officials and police became corrupt/many ordinary people were prepared to break this law.

2   By 1925, the KKK claimed to have almost five million members – mostly in the South. More importantly, many law officials were sympathisers or even members.

From boom to bust

Hoover was president when the Wall Street Crash took place and the Depression began. The source shows that the number and the percentage of unemployed grew every year (apart from 1929, for which there are no figures). From the source, we can see that the percentage went from 4.4 per cent in 1928 to 25 per cent in 1933. From this, it seems as if the actions Hoover took were not enough or did not work – in fact, he didn't begin to do anything until 1930, as he believed in the policies of laissez-faire and rugged individualism. However, the source doesn't tell us what Hoover actually did.

Roosevelt and the New Deal

1   Radicals, such as Huey Long (who began a 'Share Our Wealth' campaign) and Dr Frances Townsend, opposed the New Deal because they believed it was not doing enough to help poor people (e.g. not doing enough to improve rights at work, allowing women and African-Americans to receive unequal wages, destroying food and so pushing up prices). Communists and socialists also campaigned for a redistribution of wealth from the rich to the poor.

2   A second New Deal was needed as several of Roosevelt's first laws (e.g. NIRA in 1935 and the AAA in 1936) had been ruled unconstitutional by the Supreme Court. Also, more laws were needed to cope with the continuing problems caused by the Depression (e.g. the Social Security Act to make sure people wouldn't be dependent on charity in the future). Another reason was that although the first laws helped with some of the worst problems resulting from the Depression, they did not end it. In fact, even after the second New Deal, unemployment did not really drop to low levels until 1939 and after, when the USA began to produce weapons because of the Second World War.

From Depression to war

The graph shows that although the New Deal did help to reduce unemployment, the biggest factor in this drop was probably the outbreak of war in 1939. In 1933, 24.9 per cent of the labour force were unemployed, and this was the worst time of the Depression. Once Roosevelt took over in March 1933, he began his New Deal policies. Despite opposition from the Supreme Court and wealthy businessmen, the New Deal began to reduce unemployment – it fell every year according to the chart and, by 1937, had dropped to 14.3 per cent. However, unemployment then began to rise again during a second depression and reached 19 per cent in 1938. After that, unemployment continued to drop – especially after the start of the Second World War. Once the USA joined the war, unemployment dropped even further. By 1942, it was down to 4.7 per cent – lower than it had been in 1929.

Section 6: THE SECOND WORLD WAR, 1939–45

Causes of the war
1 He ordered the reoccupation of the Rhineland.
2 Austria

Final steps to war
1 These were the Sudeten Germans who lived in the area of Czechoslovakia known as the Sudetenland – before 1919, this had been part of the Austro-Hungarian empire.
2 This was the agreement reached by Britain, France, Italy and Germany in September 1938 that Germany should have the Sudetenland. The Czechs and the Russians (who had promised to take action to prevent this, if Britain and France also joined in) were not consulted.

Early stages
1 There were several reasons why Operation Barbarossa wasn't successful. One was that the Soviets adopted a scorched earth policy as they retreated deep into the USSR – this denied the Germans supplies. The Germans' long supply lines were then attacked by partisans. Also, the German attack had been delayed and so the army was not equipped for winter warfare (for example, they had no winter uniforms, or antifreeze for engines). Finally, the winter of 1941–2 was particularly severe.
2 Hitler was so determined to defeat the Soviet Union that he devoted 75 per cent of his armed forces to the Eastern Front, and refused to withdraw troops even when his generals told him they would be defeated. Over 90 per cent of Germany's total military casualties took place on the Eastern Front – the loss of Germany's Sixth Army at Stalingrad was a turning point that 'tore the guts out of the German army' and eventually allowed an Allied invasion of Nazi-occupied Western Europe (D-Day).

The tide begins to turn
1 This was done to help the Italians control North Africa, and especially for the campaign to capture the Suez Canal, which was a vital shipping route for Britain (especially oil).
2 The invasion of Sicily in July and then of mainland Italy in September followed by Operation Torch.

The closing stages
It shows that the US military leaders had different attitudes. Some, like Admiral Leahy, were against, while others (probably most) were in favour – this was why the decision was finally taken to drop the A-bombs.

Section 7: SUPERPOWER RELATIONS SINCE 1945

The early stages of the Cold War
For the first two conferences, the USA had been represented by Roosevelt, who was prepared to accept some of Stalin's security fears. At Tehran, there was outline agreement on redrawing the borders of Poland (through which the USSR had been invaded three times since 1900) and on the need to prevent anti-Soviet alliances in Eastern Europe. These were confirmed at Yalta, along with an initial agreement that Germany should pay reparations to the USSR for the massive damage that had been done. However, Roosevelt then died and was replaced by Truman, who was more anti-Communist – one of his first decisions at Potsdam was to oppose the idea of German reparations.

The Cold War begins
1 The four aims were to: reduce the appeal of Communism by quickly raising living standards/ rebuild Germany/weaken Soviet control of Eastern Europe/help the US economy by increasing trade with, and expanding in, Europe.
2 Although at first the USSR and some other Eastern European countries did apply for Marshall Aid, Stalin eventually withdrew the applications. This was because the conditions the USA imposed included US supervision of how the aid was spent, and that companies should be privately owned. The US government had calculated from the beginning that Stalin would find these conditions unacceptable.

Increasing tensions, 1946–9
1 Because so much of Soviet industry, agriculture, housing, roads and railways had been destroyed during the Nazi invasion – mostly by the German armed forces, which either simply destroyed factories, or stripped them of machinery, which was then shipped back to Germany. Some had also been destroyed in the 'Scorched Earth' policy, while almost 25 million Russians had died during the war. Most of the gains made during the Five-Year Plans had been wiped out – the USSR had suffered more destruction than any other country. Stalin was also worried by US plans to rebuild Germany.
2 Germany became split into two states – West and East/the USA became head of NATO, an anti-Soviet alliance.

Hot spots (1)
Source A is useful as it refers to the domino theory, which was related to the Truman Doctrine of 1947 – this was intended to stop the spread of Communism. It also shows the dates of the Soviet take-over of East European countries after 1945, which played a part in forming US foreign policy. Source B is useful as it is an extract from the US President, who was in a position to know. It also ties in with Source A and the policy of 'containment'.

However, the sources only give information about US motives for involvement up to 1950. They don't say anything about how motives and policies changed during the Korean War, which lasted until 1953. Although at first, the USA just tried to prevent Communism spreading to South Korea, its policy changed to trying to overthrow the North Korean government. Also, Source B is from a speech made during the Cold War, so it is possible that a US president would not reveal all his motives and might, in fact, be hiding something, or trying to get public support for his actions.

Hot spots (2)

1 It showed how unsuccessful US intervention had been, and began to lead some US politicians (such as Nixon) to try to find a way of withdrawing.

2 There was growing opposition to the war and US methods, in the USA and abroad, especially to the use of napalm and defoliants (e.g. 'Agent Orange') and the search-and-destroy missions (e.g. the My Lai massacre)/the morale of US troops was disintegrating/the war was causing economic and social problems in the USA/the great determination and skill of the Viet Cong and North Vietnamese troops who were experienced in guerrilla warfare.

Fluctuations

One reason was that the USSR feared that Dubček, or a successor, might take Czechoslovakia out of the Warsaw Pact, which the USSR had seen as vital for its defence ever since it had been set up in 1955. In fact, ever since 1945 and the start of the Cold War, the USSR had been determined to maintain a buffer zone in Eastern Europe. Another, more short-term reason was that Soviet, and some Eastern European, leaders were opposed to Dubček's 'Socialism with a human face' reforms (for example, a free media, the right to criticise) and feared they might spread to their own countries. They were determined to maintain their rule, so they finally sent in troops to overthrow Dubček and his supporters.

The end of the Cold War

1 Gorbachev believed that the attempt to try to keep up with the USA was ruining the Soviet economy – this was because the USA was much wealthier, so the USSR had to spend a much bigger proportion of its national income just to match US spending (25 per cent compared to 7 per cent). He also wanted to use the money saved to modernise Soviet industry and improve living standards in the USSR. He also believed the nuclear arms race was too dangerous for the world as a whole.

2 An attempted coup took place against Gorbachev by hard-line Communists in August 1991 – this led Russia, and two other republics (Belarus and the Ukraine) to set up the Commonwealth of Independent States (CIS) instead, in December 1991.

Section 8: THE USA, 1945–75

McCarthyism and the Red Scare

1 The USSR's explosion of its first nuclear weapon/the Communist Revolution in China

2 Hollywood actors, writers and directors who refused to testify to HUAC, and were eventually sent to prison

The Civil Rights Movement, 1945–62

1 Congress of Racial Equality; the Student Non-Violent Coordinating Committtee

2 The black woman whose protest began the Montgomery Bus Boycott, 1957–8

The Civil Rights Movement, 1963–75

1 Civil rights campaigners who drove buses into the Southern states to check up on whether desegregation of bus stations was being carried out, following a Supreme Court ruling

2 August 1963, at the end of the March on Washington

Other inequalities and protests

1 1924

2 Betty Freidan

Section 9: BRITAIN, 1900–14

The Liberal era begins

Both Sources A and B are clearly about poverty in Britain – Source A shows a slum in Sunderland, while Source B gives statistics about the extent of poverty. However, Source A is only one photograph and may not be typical of Sunderland, let alone the rest of the country. Whereas Source B gives figures to show how great a proportion of people were living in poverty – we can get no idea of numbers from Source A.

Problems

As this poster was produced by the WSPU it cannot be fully trusted as it is likely to be biased against the Liberal government, and will try to make it seem as horrible and cruel as possible. However, force-feeding was unpleasant and even dangerous. Sometimes, the tube missed the stomach and instead put liquid into the lungs – some Suffragettes suffered serious health problems afterwards. In 1913, the government stopped force-feeding and, instead, used the Cat and Mouse Act of 1913 to deal with those on hunger strike.

The reforms continue

This source says the Act was introduced by Lloyd George (who was the Chancellor in the Liberal government – and a supporter of New Liberalism). It also says it would give insurance cover to workers for sickness and disablement. The government, the employer and the worker each paid a regular National Insurance contribution, and it covered all workers between the age of 16 and 70 – although those who earned more than £160 a year could opt out. This was the first time most workers were covered in this way – it also gave short-term (13 weeks) unemployment benefit, but only for the low paid, and not for those in industries such as building and engineering, which often suffered unemployment. It was the start of the Welfare State, and was based on similar schemes that had been introduced earlier in Germany.

Section 10: BRITAIN, 1914–18

Winning minds

This source is useful as it was written by someone who was a soldier in the First World War, and who therefore knew about the conditions. However, this is only one man's view, and it doesn't give any indication of how many others felt this way. However, there were many opposed to the war – even from the start in 1914. In particular, there were about 16 000 conscientious objectors in Britain – about half of these refused to do any war work and 6000 were sent to prison. As the war went on, many came to think like Sassoon – this was one reason conscription had to be introduced in 1916.

The home front (1)

1 To prevent spying/defend against invasion/ increase war production/ensure there was enough food

2 DORA allowed the government to take over factories for war production, and set up a Ministry of Munitions to control the production of weapons and ammunition. British Summer Time was brought in to give an extra hour of work time, and the opening hours of pubs were reduced in an attempt to prevent drunkenness and absenteeism.

The home front (2)

1 This was before the introduction of conscription in 1916, and was done to shame men into volunteering, by saying they were cowards.

2 Because so many men were conscripted, there was a serious labour shortage – especially in war-related jobs such as engineering and munitions. In order to win such a 'total' war, it was necessary to employ large numbers of women.

3 Women were seen as having played an important part in Britain's victory, and had showed they were capable of doing many jobs that previously had been male-only jobs. In 1918, women over the age of 30 were given the vote (although full voting equality was not achieved until 1928). But most women returned to traditional roles after the war.

Section 11: BRITAIN, 1918–39

Impact of the First World War

1 These were the traditional/establised industries, such as coal, iron, steel, shipbuilding, engineering and textiles.

2 3026 million metres

3 Any two from: loss of markets during the war/loss of wartime contracts after 1918/ increased competition from abroad (especially the USA, Germany and Japan)/lack of investment in modern machinery and industries

Political and economic problems

1 Because their uniform was a mixture of police (black) and army (khaki/tan) clothes

2 The caption says the dead person was a Sinn Fein suspect. There is no weapon by him – so if they had shot him when he was unarmed, then it shows the Black and Tans were ruthless. One of the Black and Tans is also pointing a cocked revolver at the other suspect. However, this is only one photograph – although the Black and Tans were often violent, there is not enough evidence here to prove they were.

Britain in the 1930s

Source A is an official report about poverty and malnutrition in South Wales in 1932–3; it says that the 'economic depression has undoubtedly lowered the standard of living in many homes' and so led to increased malnutrition. This backs up Source B, published in 1937 during the Depression, which gives details of the poverty and poor diet suffered by the family of an unemployed miner, which results in 'physical degeneracy' – this is possibly the same thing as the malnutrition in Source A.

However, Source A says that there were other causes of the malnutrition, which had existed before the Depression, while Source B doesn't even mention the Depression, just unemployment – although unemployment rose greatly because of the Depression in the 1930s.

Section 12: BRITAIN, 1939–45

Britain and the start of the war

1 Dads' Army

2 They were to help resist the expected German invasion: their main jobs were to guard the coasts, roadblocks and telephone exchanges.

The war at home

1 These were official outdoor air-raid shelters issued by the government, to be put in people's gardens. They were made of corrugated steel, and were sunk in the ground about one metre deep, and then covered with soil, with a steel shield for the door and a blast wall for extra protection.

2 The sources show that civilians were deliberately targeted, and that many were killed in the Blitz. This was despite the shelters provided by the government, like those in Source A that are being delivered to an ordinary street. Source B gives an indication of civilian casualties, and also tells us that civilians were involved in rescuing corpses from the rubble.

Women and the 'double burden'

Women played a variety of roles in the Second World War. At first, they were encouraged to volunteer for the women's sections of the armed forces or to do war work. Then in 1941, all single women, aged 19–30, were conscripted for these tasks. Source A shows some of the 30 000 women who did agricultural work, as members of the Women's Land Army. Others worked in munitions factories or other factories connected to war production (for example, medical supplies, uniforms). Others drove lorries, trams and buses, or worked on the railways. Many worked in offices, the civil service and the Post Office.

Many women joined the women's sections of the armed forces (WRNS, WRAF or the WRAC), while others joined the ATS, the Civil Defence organisations or acted as ARP wardens. Generally, they were not involved in combat – although some members of the ATA trained as pilots and flew planes from the factories to the air bases. However, as Source B shows, there was an exception with the SOE: this was the only organisation that gave women the same training as men, and allowed them to take part in military combat (mainly as secret agents in France).

Section 13: BRITAIN, 1945–79

Labour's Welfare State

The message of the cartoon seems to be that the doctors do not like the National Health Service, and that Anuerin Bevan (he has 'AB' on his hat) is forcing them to take it. The cartoon is from 1948, when the newly elected Labour government first introduced the NHS on 5 July. Before then, people had to pay for all medical services. When Labour said it was going to introduce a free health service – as recommended by the 1942 Beveridge Report – many doctors objected, fearing loss of the money that they earned from private fees and a reduction of professional independence. Anuerin Bevan, the Minister for Health, made some concessions, but insisted that there would be a free health service for all. Many doctors, including many GPs, were still unhappy (hence the caption: 'It still tastes awful.').

Politics and society

1 1958
2 Northern Ireland Civil Rights Association (NICRA)

Britain's economy – boom and bust

Source A should be accurate as it is a photograph taken in June 1977. It shows a protest that needed a lot of police. However, it is only one photograph, and there is nothing to show that the protest is about trade unions. However, there was a long dispute over the rights of workers to belong to trade unions at Grunwick's photo-processing plant, and the workers were angry about strike-breakers being bussed in with police protection. Source B is a cartoon which says that trade unions have helped to bring down two governments – its purpose may be to turn people against trade unions as, by 1979, many people were against unions and the many strikes (such as the one shown in Source A), so it may be biased and therefore not very accurate. However, during the 1970s, there were problems in industrial relations, and miners' strikes in 1972 and 1974 are believed by many historians to have played a part in the downfall of Edward Heath's (the first 'head') Conservative government in February 1974, while James Callaghan's (the second 'head') Labour government lost the 1979 election partly because of the 'Winter of Discontent', when many unions went on strike over pay. So Source B is probably more accurate than Source A – even though it is a cartoon, it was published in a newspaper that was not particularly anti-trade union.

Britain and the world

1 Nationalist movements and decolonisation in the British Empire
2 1972

Women in the 1950s

1 It resulted in longer life expectancies and so spending a relatively shorter part of their lives being pregnant or looking after young children.
2 Domestic science

Women's liberation in the 1960s

There were several demands raised by feminists in Britain during the 1960s – most of which were to do with equality, rather than the radical political beliefs shown in Source A. The main demands were for equal opportunities in education in schools (such as not having separate subjects for girls, e.g. domestic science), access to universities and equal employment and pay prospects. Feminists were especially angered by the glass ceiling that seemed to prevent promotion to top jobs – a report by the NCCL in 1964 showed how few women got into the top professions. Some were also beginning to question the traditional housewife/mother role.

Equality in the 1970s?

Both sources are photographs – but only Source A says it is from the 1970s. However, both contain information that is useful. Source A mentions abortion, and shows a banner with the Women's Liberation symbol – abortion on demand was a key demand of the Women's Liberation Movement. Source B is also useful as it refers to the criticisms made by Women's Liberation groups about how the traditional housewife/mother role traps women into subservient positions in relation to men.

However, neither of these two sources refer to all of the main demands of the Women's Liberation Movement in the 1970s. These were set out after they held a National Conference in 1970 and drew up four main demands – and include demands for equal pay, equal education and opportunity, 24-hour nurseries and free contraception (as well as abortion). Later, the Women's Liberation Movement took up the issue of domestic violence – with Erin Pizzey setting up the first refuge for battered wives in 1971, in Chiswick. These are not mentioned by the two sources, but, as Source A says it is from the 1970s, this makes it more useful than Source B.

Key terms

Section 1: THE FIRST WORLD WAR, 1890–1918

armistice ceasefire – the end of the fighting in the First World War

Balkans the area of south-east Europe that includes countries such as Greece, Bulgaria, Serbia and Romania

colonies countries conquered by other more powerful ones, which are then made part of the conquering country's empire

conscientious objectors people who refused to join the army on moral or religious grounds, sometimes called 'conchies'

conscription when people are forced by law to join the armed services, and possibly imprisoned if they refuse

convoy system merchant ships sailing together in a zigzag pattern, protected by destroyers

dreadnoughts large battleships built by Britain and Germany in the naval race that developed after 1900

entente French word meaning 'understanding' – hence 'Entente Cordiale' and the 'Triple Entente'

going over the top troops advancing out of their trenches en masse

Great Powers most powerful countries of Europe (Britain, France, Russia and – after 1871 – Germany)

hydrophones equipment used to detect submarines

Kaiser German emperor – from the word 'Caesar'

nationalism a strong identity with a particular people, culture and language – and the desire to be joined together in a united and independent country

no-man's land ground between two opposing front lines, controlled by neither side

propaganda use of the media (for example, songs, newspapers, posters) to put forward a particular point of view

race to the sea race to capture the Channel ports in the First World War

reserved occupations jobs that were exempt from conscription, such as miners, farmers, etc.

U-boats German submarines

war of attrition to win by destroying more enemy forces, whatever the losses of one's own troops, and so wear down the other side

Zeppelins German airships used to bomb British cities in the First World War

Section 2: THE LEAGUE OF NATIONS, 1919–39

Articles of the Covenant rules that governed the League of Nations

Big Three victors of the First World War – the USA, France and Britain

isolationism policy of non-involvement in world affairs practised by the USA between the First and Second World Wars

League of Nations formed after the First World War to help prevent another world war, similar to the United Nations

November Criminals name given by ordinary Germans to German politicians who signed the armistice in 1918, and the subsequent Versailles peace treaty in 1919

reparations compensation money Germany had to pay for 'causing' the First World War

Treaty of Versailles signed at the end of the First World War between the Allies and Germany

War Guilt Clause the part of the Treaty of Versailles in which Germany accepted responsibility for starting the First World War

Section 3: RUSSIA IN REVOLUTION, 1917–41

Bolsheviks group of Russian revolutionaries led by Lenin who gained power in 1917

collectivisation system in which small private farms were merged into larger state farms

commissar title given to ministers in the revolutionary Bolshevik government

Five-Year Plans drawn up under Stalin to speed up industrialisation of the USSR

kulaks better-off peasants

NEP New Economic Policy – Lenin's economic reforms to ensure an adequate food supply after the failure of War Communism

purges murder or imprisonment by Stalin of leading Bolsheviks and many millions of officials and army officers

Red Army the Bolshevik army

show trials trials based on little or no evidence designed to convict leading Bolsheviks during Stalin's rule

War Communism emergency economic measures carried out by the Bolsheviks, 1917–21

White armies anti-Bolsheviks supported by foreign powers

Section 4: GERMANY, 1918–45

Aryan a white person of non-Jewish descent

chancellor head of the German government

depression high unemployment and mass hardship

Final Solution Nazi policy to wipe out the Jewish race in Europe

hyperinflation vast increase in the cost of living due to the devaluation of the mark

Kristallnacht Crystal Night, or Night of Broken Glass, when thousands of Jewish businesses were destroyed

Nazi a member of the National Socialist German Workers' Party (NSDAP)

Night of the Long Knives purge of the SA (Brownshirts) by Hitler

Putsch sudden attempt to remove a government by force

Section 5: THE USA, 1919–45

buying on the margin buying shares with a 10 per cent deposit and being given credit for the rest

federal central (for example, federal government)

HP Hire Purchase

laissez-faire letting businesses operate with no government controls

lame duck months the time when a president had been elected, but had not yet taken office

rugged individualism people helping themselves without government assistance

Supreme Court the highest court in the USA

tariff import duty

Section 6: THE SECOND WORLD WAR, 1939–45

Anschluss union (particularly in relation to Germany's union with Austria)

appeasement making concessions to aggressive countries to avoid war

Axis the alliance between a number of Fascist states in the lead-up to the Second World War

Blitzkrieg lightning war

Comintern Communist International

Lebensraum a German term that means 'living space'

partisan guerrilla

Phoney War first few months of the Second World War when no serious conflict between Germany and Britain took place

Plebiscite referendum, or vote, of the people on a particular issue

scorched earth policy policy of burning crops and buildings in order to deny supplies to an enemy

ultimatum final demand or threat

Section 7: SUPERPOWER RELATIONS SINCE 1945

Cold War the rivalry and tension between the capitalist West and Communist East after the Second World War

contain stop

domino theory American theory that if one country becomes Communist, its neighbours will follow suit

imperialist wanting to dominate the world with economic and military power

Iron Curtain imaginary line between Communist Eastern Europe and capitalist Western Europe

Marshall Plan American economic plan for the reconstruction of Europe after the Second World War

reparations compensation

satellite client or subordinate (for example, satellite state)

summit meeting

veto block or prevent

Warsaw Pact treaty between Communist European countries

Section 8: THE USA, 1945–75

Black Power the belief that the answer to racial discrimination, segregation and violence should be black people organising themselves, without relying on sympathetic whites; and that violence should be met with violence

Black Panthers a Black Power group set up by Huey Newton and Bobby Seale

boycott a form of direct action that involves not buying particular products, or refusing to use certain shops, services, etc. in protest against certain policies

civil rights the basic human rights of a citizen to equal treatment and opportunities, regardless of race, gender, class, sexual orientation or age (e.g. in employment, education, public services) and the right to vote in elections

Cold War the hostile relations that existed after 1945 between the capitalist USA and the Communist Soviet Union

draft term used for conscription in the USA – draft cards were sent to those being called up

feminism the movement that struggled to achieve equality for women, and challenged traditional 'male' concepts of what a woman's role should be

Freedom Rides the bus journeys taken by civil rights campaigners to check that desegregation was being carried out in the Southern states of the USA

Hispanic-Americans Americans whose origins are in Spanish-speaking countries, such as Mexico, Puerto Rico and Cuba

HUAC the House Committee on Un-American Activities, which investigated people for their Communist beliefs or associations

Jim Crow laws the racist laws that existed in the Southern states of the USA to enforce discrimination and segregation against black Americans. The term originated from a character created by a white racist comedian

male chauvinism beliefs held by some men about the 'natural', or inherent, superiority of men and the inferiority of women – often used to justify inequalities regarding pay, education, employment, etc.

McCarthyism the hysteria surrounding the anti-Communist witch-hunts in the USA during the late 1940s and the early 1950s, which resulted from Senator McCarthy's claims about Communist spies

Native Americans people and their descendants (e.g. Sioux, Cheyennes, Creeks) who were living in America before the first Europeans arrived – often known as 'Indians' or 'Red Indians'

non-violent direct action forms of protest used by those who refuse to respond violently to any violence inflicted on them (e.g. sit-ins, sit-downs, boycotts, marches)

Red Scare periods in the USA when the authorities and the media ran campaigns against those individuals and groups with radical or left-wing views (e.g. anarchists, socialists and Communists)

segregation separation of different races or ethnic groups (e.g. having separate schools, hospitals, transport, restaurants), with the subordinate groups receiving inferior treatment and services

sit-in form of non-violent direct action or protest that involves simply sitting down in a building or room and refusing to move – even if violence or arrest follows

Swinging Sixties the 1960s, which were associated with greater freedoms, a more relaxed attitude to sex and drugs by many younger people, the explosion of rock music, the hippies and political protests

Women's Liberation Movement the organisations set up by feminists from the mid-1960s to achieve full equality for women, and to challenge male chauvinism and sexism towards women

Section 9–12: BRITAIN, 1900–45

black market illegal trading of shortage items (especially food) – at high prices

blackout a system to ensure no lights from houses, street lamps, etc. showed at night, so that bombers had no help in finding targets

Blitz the bombing of London and other British cities, 1940–1

conscientious objector a man or woman whose principles are opposed to fighting in a war, or helping the war effort

conscription compulsory military service – failure to report for duty was a criminal offence

general strike a national strike in which all unions and workers in a country go on strike

home rule self-government for Ireland in most matters (for example, education, welfare, taxation), but with Britain in charge of the police, foreign policy and defence. Many Irish Nationalists wanted this, but militant Republicans wanted total independence

National Government The name of the coalition government formed in 1931, by the Labour Prime Minister, Ramsay MacDonald – it soon became dominated by the Conservatives

nationalisation a form of social (as opposed to private) ownership of industry, banks, etc., in which the government takes over and runs the relevant parts of the economy

New Liberalism ideas in the early twentieth century about social welfare reforms and the formation of a welfare state – influenced by the reports about poverty in Britain by Booth, Rowntree and Beveridge, and by the social welfare system in Germany

partition this means division, and refers to the splitting of Ireland into North and South in 1922

protectionism the attempt to protect national industries by placing tariffs (customs duties) on imported/foreign goods

Scramble for Africa the last spurt of imperialism when, in the late nineteenth century, Britain, France, Germany and other European countries raced to colonise Africa, and so increase their empires

staple industries these were the 'old' established industries in Britain (for example, coal, engineering and textiles) – these suffered from under-investment by their private owners and increased foreign competition, especially after the First World War

syndicalism a revolutionary anarchist idea, based on the belief that industries should be owned and run by the people who work in them. Its main leader was Tom Mann, and it was especially influential amongst workers in the years 1910–14

Triple Industrial Alliance formed by the three biggest trade unions (the miners, transport workers and the railwaymen) in 1913, against what was seen as a joint campaign by employers and the state to defeat legal strikes

welfare state a system by which the government helps provide health care, social security and education for all its citizens, financed by contributions (National Insurance) and taxation – with the wealthy contributing to the welfare of the less well-off

Section 13: BRITAIN, 1945–79

B Specials the all-Protestant armed police force set up in Northern Ireland after Partition, under the Special Powers Act

balance of payments the difference between the cost of a country's imports and its income from exports

battered wives a term used to describe women who suffer physical abuse from their husbands

Beveridge Report a report published in 1942, recommending ways to tackle the 'five giants' of Want (poverty), Disease, Ignorance (education), Squalor (poor housing) and Idleness (unemployment)

Bloody Sunday 31 January 1972, the day British paratroopers shot dead thiteen civil rights protesters in Londonderry

Clause 4 the part of the 1918 Labour Party constitution that called for social or public ownership of banks and factories

CND Campaign for Nuclear Disarmament: the anti-nuclear weapons movement that was set up in the 1950s

Direct Rule when the British government suspended the government and parliament of Northern Ireland (Stormont) in 1972 and ruled the province directly from Westminster

EEC the European and Economic Community – now known as the European Union

feminism the ideas and movement that challenged male attitudes to women, and which struggled for equality

gerrymandering the process in Northern Ireland by which the Protestant authorities fixed election boundaries to ensure Unionist (Protestant) candidates stood better chances of winning local elections

glass ceiling the invisible 'block' of discrimination that prevents women from getting promotion to the best jobs

immigration the movement of people leaving one country to find work and a better life in a new country

internment imprisonment without trial, introduced in Northern Ireland in 1971 as a way of dealing with the Troubles, which had broken out in the 1960s

nationalisation when a government takes an industry into public ownership and control, paying compensation to the former private owners

Orange Order a Protestant organisation (named after the Protestant king of Britain, William III of Orange), set up in the 1790s to protect against what they saw as the threat from Catholicism; by the 1960s, almost 100 000 Protestants belonged to the Orange Order, which organised marches every July to commemorate the victory won by William III in 1690

refuge a place where women and children fleeing domestic violence could find safety – the first one was set up in Chiswick by Erin Pizzey in 1971

Republicans people (mostly Catholic) in Northern Ireland who want Ireland to be one united country that is not ruled by Great Britain – an alternative name is 'Nationalists'

socialism the political belief that the main parts of a country's economy (banks, industries, mines) should be socially owned and controlled in order to create a fairer and more equal society – based on the belief that capitalism (private ownership) creates deep inequalities, divisions and exploitation

special relationship refers to the close political and military ties and cooperation said to exist between the USA and Britain, based on shared values

Stormont the place in Belfast where the parliament and government of Northern Ireland are based

Unionists people (mostly Protestant) who want Northern Ireland to remain part of the United Kingdom and so oppose a united Irish Republic (sometimes known as Loyalists, because they remain loyal to the British crown)

wage freeze a government incomes policy designed to control inflation, which tries to set limits to – or even prevent – wage increases; sometimes, but not always, accompanied by limits on price increases

welfare state the idea that the state should provide, via taxation, sufficient public facilities and services (such as medical care, old age pensions, education and other state benefits), to ensure that no one lives in poverty and that all have equal opportunities

Zionism a movement, set up in the nineteenth century, which believes that Jews should have their own homeland in order to avoid persecution. Several places were originally considered, but eventually Palestine was chosen – even though most of its inhabitants were Palestinian Arabs. After 1945, some Zionist groups used terrorism against the British authorities and the local Arabs in order to set up the new state of Israel in what had been Palestine.

Last-minute learner

- **These seven pages give you the most important facts across the whole subject in the smallest possible space.**
- **You can use these pages as a final check.**
- **You can also use them as you revise as a way to check your learning.**
- **You can cut them out for quick and easy reference.**

Section 1: The First World War, 1890–1918

1890–1914
- After the defeat of France in the Franco-Prussian War of 1870–1, and the subsequent creation of Germany in 1871, tensions arose between the Great Powers over trade and colonies – especially in Africa.
- This resulted in arms races between the Great Powers and the creation of alliance systems, which only increased the tensions.
- Nationalism in the Balkans after 1900 began to drag some of the Great Powers, such as Austria–Hungary and Russia, into new crises – especially after Bosnia–Herzegovina was annexed by Austria–Hungary in 1908.

1914–16
- The assassination in Sarajevo, June 1914, and the alliance system, resulted in war in August.
- Both sides expected a short war, but it soon settled into stalemate (trench warfare and a war of attrition).
- New weapons failed to end the deadlock.

1917–18
- In April 1917, the USA joined the Allies, although Russia later dropped out.
- The Germans launched a Spring Offensive in March 1918. Although successful at first, it failed.
- After August 1918, the Allies counter-attacked. Mutinies and unrest in Germany forced the Kaiser to abdicate.
- A new provisional government in Germany signed an armistice on 11 November, and the war ended.

1918–19
- In January 1918, Wilson issued his Fourteen Points.
- In January 1919, the Allies met in Paris to discuss peace – without the defeated powers.

1919–20
- The 'Big Three' drew up the Treaty of Versailles, which the Germans signed under duress.
- The treaty imposed many territorial losses and military restrictions. Unification with Austria was forbidden. The 'War Guilt Clause' obliged Germany to pay reparations.
- Treaties were also signed with the other defeated Central Powers. These, too, involved the transfer of land and people, along with military restrictions and, for some, the payment of compensation.
- This led to economic dislocation and ethnic unrest in the Successor States.

1921–3
- In 1921, the Reparations Committee decided Germany should pay £6600 million in compensation.
- A nationalist revolt in Turkey forced the Allies to sign a new treaty (Lausanne) in 1923.

Section 2: The League of Nations, 1919–39

1919–20
- Wilson of the USA persuaded the Allies to set up the League of Nations.
- Its main aims were to protect the independence of all countries, and to bring about disarmament.
- Decisions had to be unanimous, and its main power was economic sanctions. It did not have its own military force.
- The USA decided not to join, while Germany and its former allies were temporarily excluded. Communist Russia was not invited to join.
- The headquarters of the League were in Geneva. There was an Assembly, a permanent Council, a Secretariat, and several special commissions. The League's first meeting was in 1920.

1920–9
- The League had several successes in solving disputes involving smaller countries. Its commissions dealt with refugees, diseases and working conditions.
- However, it failed to bring about disarmament and to solve several important disputes that involved the more powerful members of the League.
- In 1926, Germany was allowed to join the League.
- Several non-League agreements were made: the Dawes Plan, 1924; the Locarno Treaty, 1925; the Kellogg-Briand Pact, 1928; the Young Plan, 1929.
- Nonetheless, by 1929, the League had played an important part in promoting co-operation and the peaceful settling of disputes.

1929–39
- After the start of the Great Depression in 1929, many countries adopted a more aggressive foreign policy. Despite some successes, the League was increasingly ignored.
- The two main crises were the Japanese invasion of Manchuria in 1931 and the Italian invasion of Abyssinia in 1935.
- In both cases, the League failed to prevent aggression.
- The World Disarmament Conference, 1932–3, was also a failure.

Section 3: Russia in revolution, 1917–41

1900–17

- In 1900, the Russian empire was ruled by Nicholas II, an all-powerful tsar. But there were various political opposition groups. An attempt at revolution in 1905 failed, and the Tsar's rule seemed secure after he agreed to some reforms that helped better-off peasants and set up a Duma (parliament).
- Russia's involvement in the First World War produced a crisis in 1917. After the March Revolution, the Tsar abdicated and a Provisional Government took over. Unrest continued and, in April, Lenin returned. In November, the Bolsheviks overthrew the Provisional Government and power passed to the All-Russian Congress of Soviets.

1918–24

- A newly elected Constituent Assembly was dismissed in January 1918, and in March the Treaty of Brest-Litovsk ended Russia's part in the First World War.
- This peace ended the Bolshevik coalition with the Left SRs. A civil war broke out between the Reds (Communists) and the Whites (anti-Communists). Although many foreign countries intervened to help the Whites, Trotsky created a Red Army that eventually won the war.
- However, to fight the war, Lenin's government was forced to take emergency economic measures known as War Communism. This was unpopular and provoked the serious Kronstadt Rebellion in 1921; it was replaced by a New Economic Policy, which slowly improved the economy.
- In 1922, Lenin suffered the first of several strokes, and he died in 1924.

1924–9

- Before he died, Lenin wrote his 'Last Testament'; in 1923, he added a 'Postscript' in which he recommended Stalin be removed from power.
- After Lenin's death, a struggle for power began. Zinoviev and Kamenev joined Stalin to prevent Trotsky becoming the next leader. However, Stalin used his position to remove Zinoviev and Kamenev from the party, as well as to expel Trotsky.
- To do this, Stalin allied with Bukharin and the Right. As soon as the Left and United Oppositions had been defeated, Stalin turned on Bukharin. By 1929, Stalin had defeated all his main rivals.

1929–41

- Stalin now decided to modernise the Soviet economy. He wanted to rapidly expand Soviet industry – to do this, he had to make Soviet farming much more efficient.
- In agriculture, he introduced forced collectivisation. This met with much opposition from the kulaks. At first, this led to a serious decline in production.
- Soviet industry was transformed by the Five-Year Plans. These concentrated mostly on heavy industry.
- Stalin also began a Great Purge of the Communist Party and the armed forces. A series of show trials led to the execution of all his main opponents. Several million victims ended up in the gulags.
- After 1933, Stalin feared attack from Nazi Germany. The USSR joined the League of Nations in 1934, but failed to secure an alliance with Britain and France. So, in 1939, Stalin signed a non-aggression pact with Hitler.

Section 4: Germany, 1918–45

1918–23

- In October, the Kiel mutiny led to revolution, and the new provisional government signed an armistice in November 1918. The left-wing Spartacist Revolt was crushed by the army and the Freikorps.
- The Weimar Republic was set up in 1919, with a new democratic constitution. In 1920, the Nazi Party was formed.
- The terms of the Treaty of Versailles and the introduction of democracy led to much opposition from the conservative and nationalist right, including Kapp's Putsch, 1920.
- When Germany fell behind with reparation payments, the French occupied the Ruhr in 1923. This led to economic collapse and hyperinflation. The Nazis' Beer Hall Putsch in Munich failed, and Hitler was imprisoned.

1924–9

- The German economy recovered under Stresemann. Reparation payments were reduced by the Dawes and Young Plans, negotiated with the USA.
- Germany signed the Locarno Treaty, joined the League of Nations, and signed the Kellogg–Briand Pact.
- As a result, support for extremist political parties declined during these 'Golden Years'. After release from prison, Hitler began to reorganise the Nazi Party.
- In October 1929, Stresemann died; then the Wall Street Crash in the USA led to the Great Depression. Loans from the USA stopped, and unemployment in Germany rose rapidly.

1930–3

- By 1932, six million people were unemployed; Nazi support increased. Hindenburg increasingly ruled by decree.

- Hitler reassured wealthy industrialists that the Nazis had no intention of implementing the 'socialist' parts of their programme, and donations to the Nazi Party increased. In July 1932, the Nazis became the largest party in the Reichstag.
- The Nazis lost seats in the November 1932 elections, while the Communists increased their share again. Von Papen persuaded Hindenburg to appoint Hitler as Chancellor on 30 January 1933.

1933–9

- Hitler immediately called for new elections in March. But the Reichstag Fire, February 1933, led to the banning of the Communists. The Enabling Act was passed: by July 1933, Germany was a one-party state.
- Terror (SS and Gestapo) and propaganda (Goebbels) were used to prevent opposition. Despite this, some individuals and groups continued to oppose the Nazis.
- Opposition from more militant Nazis was ended by the Night of the Long Knives in June 1934. In August, when Hindenburg died, the army supported Hitler becoming Führer.
- The Nazis dealt with unemployment by public works schemes. Women were pushed out of some jobs, encouraged to marry and have large families. The Nazis also tried to control young people through the Hitler Youth.
- The Nazis began their anti-Semitic policies in 1933. A boycott of Jewish shops, and the expulsion of Jews from the civil service, were followed by the Nuremberg Laws in 1935. Violence was stepped up after the Night of Broken Glass in 1938.

1939–45

- After 1939 and the start of the Second World War, Nazi policy towards the Jews became more extreme. In 1942, the Final Solution began, under SS supervision.

Section 5: The USA, 1919–45

1918–28

- The Republicans won the 1920 presidential election, and promised to return the USA to 'normalcy' in foreign affairs ('isolationism' in relation to Europe, though not the Americas and Asia) and economics (laissez-faire).
- With regard to isolationism, the USA stayed out of the League of Nations; however, it did help Germany with its reparations payments via the Dawes Plan in 1924. It also signed the Washington Treaty in 1922, to limit naval expansion.
- From 1920, the USA experienced an economic and industrial boom under the Republicans, who reduced the restrictions and taxes on big companies (the 'trusts') that the Democrats had introduced to protect ordinary people. Many ordinary people began to buy shares in companies in order to make a profit. But not all sections of US society shared in this new wealth.
- During this boom, however, there were several problems: prohibition of alcohol and the rise of gangsters; racism and violence against African-Americans by the Ku Klux Klan; restrictions on immigration; a Red Scare.

1929–33

- Herbert Hoover won the 1928 presidential election for the Republicans. But in October 1929, the collapse of the US stock market on Wall Street began the Great Depression.
- Sales fell, firms closed and unemployment soared. At first, Hoover refused to act, as he believed in 'rugged individualism'. By 1932, almost 25 per cent of American workers were unemployed.
  Although Hoover started to take some action, he lost the

November 1932 elections to the Democratic candidate, Roosevelt, who promised the American people a 'New Deal'.

1933–6

- When Roosevelt took over in March 1933, he began a series of 'fireside chats' to restore confidence, and in his 'Hundred Days' took action to strengthen the banking system. He also set up a series of 'Alphabet Agencies' to deal with the various problems.
- However, the first New Deal was opposed by both left (radicals) and right (conservatives, Republicans, 'states rights' supporters). In particular, the conservatives in the Supreme Court ruled that many of Roosevelt's policies were unconstitutional.
- Roosevelt responded by announcing a second New Deal. Despite these problems, Roosevelt won an even bigger majority in the 1936 presidential election. He then tried to get approval to add extra judges to the Supreme Court, but this was blocked by Congress.

1937–41

- As the second New Deal began to reduce unemployment, Roosevelt decided to cut government spending. But this coincided with another drop in world trade and resulted in a mini Depression in 1937–8. As a result, unemployment rose again.
- However, from 1938, Roosevelt became increasingly concerned about the approach of war in Europe, and especially about Japanese expansion in China and the Pacific. A US oil embargo on Japan was followed by the Japanese attack on Pearl Harbor in December 1941, which brought the USA into the Second World War.

Section 6: The Second World War, 1939–45

1930–5

- After the Depression, the League found it increasingly difficult to prevent aggression.
- When Japan invaded the Chinese province of Manchuria in 1931, the League was unable to take effective action.
- After Hitler came to power in 1933, the League found it even more difficult to take firm action.
- The 1932–33 World Disarmament Conference failed to reach agreement. In 1933, both Japan and Germany left the League.
- At first, Fascist Italy acted with Britain and France against Hitler. They blocked Hitler's attempt to take over Austria in 1934, and formed the Stresa Front in 1935.
- However, this alliance broke down post-1935, after Mussolini's invasion of Abyssinia. Italy began moving closer to Nazi Germany.

1936–8

- In 1936, Hitler stepped up German rearmament and reoccupied the Rhineland. Along with Mussolini, he also intervened in the Spanish Civil War. In October, Italy and Germany signed the Rome–Berlin Axis.
- Under Chamberlain, Prime Minister of Britain from 1937, the policy of appeasement was followed. In 1938, at the Munich Conference, Germany was given the Sudetenland area of Czechoslovakia. Germany's invasion of the rest of Czechoslovakia in 1939 also met no opposition. But Britain and France then promised to defend Poland.

1939–41

- In August, after several failed attempts to secure an alliance with Britain and France to oppose German

expansion, Stalin signed a non-aggression pact with Hitler.
- In September 1939, shortly after signing this, Hitler invaded Poland. Britain and France declared war on Germany.
- The 'Phoney War' saw little fighting. But in 1940, Nazi Blitzkrieg methods allowed Hitler to occupy Denmark, Norway, the Netherlands, Belgium and part of France. The BEF had to be evacuated from Dunkirk to avoid capture.
- Britain was on its own, but won the Battle of Britain and so prevented a German invasion.
- In addition to these Axis victories in the west, Italian forces inflicted early defeats on British forces in North Africa.
- In June 1941, Hitler launched a massive invasion of the Soviet Union (Operation Barbarossa).

1942–5

- In the winter of 1941, the situation started to change for the Axis powers. The Russians held on and counter-attacked, while Italian forces suffered set-backs in North Africa and the Balkans.
- In December 1941, Japan attacked Pearl Harbor and Germany declared war on the USA. In early 1942, the Allies began heavy bombing of Germany. In May 1942, early Japanese successes in the Pacific War were ended by the Battle of Midway.
- During 1943, Axis forces suffered a series of defeats in Europe (Stalingrad), North Africa (El Alamein) and the Pacific. In July, the Allied invasion of Italy began, and Mussolini was overthrown.
- The final stage of the war began with the D-Day landings in June 1944. In May 1945, Hitler committed suicide and Germany surrendered. The war in the Pacific was ended in August when the USA dropped two atomic bombs on Japan.

Section 7: Superpower relations since 1945

1943–5

- Despite tensions between the Allies, meetings in 1943 (Tehran) and 1944 (Moscow) showed some common ground.
- Differences over German reparations and Poland at the Yalta Conference, February 1945, widened at the Potsdam Conference, July–August 1945, when Truman replaced Roosevelt and the USA dropped atomic bombs on Japan.

1946–7

- In March 1946, Churchill's 'Iron Curtain' speech about the Soviet takeover of Eastern Europe marked the start of the Cold War.
- In 1947, the USA announced the Truman Doctrine and the Marshall Plan.

1948–9

- In June 1948, disagreements over Germany led to the Berlin Blockade and the Berlin Airlift.
- In April 1949, the West formed NATO, the Berlin Blockade was called off, and Germany became two separate states.
- In August, the USSR exploded its own A-bomb. In October, the Chinese Communists came to power.

1950–61

- In June 1950, the Korean War began.
- The USA got the UN to send troops to help South Korea. Eventually, in 1953, an armistice ended the fighting in Korea.
- After 1953, there was a 'thaw' in the Cold War.
- But when West Germany joined NATO in 1955, the USSR set up the Warsaw Pact Organisation.
- Relations improved after July 1955, but the Hungarian Revolt, 1956, and a new crisis over Germany and Berlin, 1958, increased tensions again. In 1961, the Berlin Wall was built.

1962–79

- The two most serious 'hot spots' were Cuba and Vietnam.
- In 1961, Kennedy's Bay of Pigs venture to overthrow Castro failed, but this led to the Cuban Missile Crisis in 1962.
- This ended when Khrushchev withdrew the missiles in return for Kennedy secretly promising not to invade Cuba and to withdraw US missiles based in Turkey.
- In 1963, the USA and USSR set up a 'hot line' and signed a Nuclear Test Ban Treaty.
- In Vietnam, because of the Cold War and the domino theory, the USA gave increasing aid to the South.
- After Kennedy's assassination in 1963, Johnson took over and US involvement in Vietnam escalated.
- In 1969, Nixon, the new president, began 'Vietnamisation', to end direct US involvement.
- The USA withdrew from Vietnam in 1973. In 1975, the North defeated the South and reunited Vietnam.
- Despite Vietnam, relations between East and West improved during the late 1960s and early 1970s (détente).
- But this was undermined by events in Czechoslovakia in 1968 and in Poland in 1980.
- Also, revolutions in the Third World in the 1970s, and Soviet intervention in Afghanistan in 1979, led US President Reagan to begin a Second Cold War, involving a new arms race.

1980–91

- In 1985, Gorbachev became the new leader of the USSR. He offered arms reduction, and said the USSR would no longer intervene in Eastern Europe.
- During 1989, Eastern European Communist governments resigned.
- A coup against Gorbachev in 1991 failed, but the Soviet Union then broke up. This marked the end of the Cold War.

Section 8: The USA, 1945–75

1945–53

- Even before the Bolshevik Revolution in Russia in 1917, the USA had been strongly opposed to left-wing ideas. A Red Scare against socialists, Communists and anarchists had developed in the 1920s.
- US opposition to Communism was temporarily reduced during the Second World War but, after 1945, broke out again in what became known as the Cold War.
- In 1949, the victory of the Chinese Communist Party, and the ending of the USA's nuclear weapons' monopoly by the USSR, increased fears about Communism.
- In this atmosphere, the US government set up the House Committee on Un-American Activities (HUAC) to examine the views and sympathies of certain people – such as Alger Hiss – to see if they were Soviet spies or Communists.
- Senator Joseph McCarthy then launched his own campaign, claiming that hundreds of Communists were working in government jobs. The hysteria that such claims led to resulted in the formation of the Tydings Committee in 1950, and created a witch-hunt that became known as 'McCarthyism' – many people lost their jobs.
- However, his constantly changing 'evidence' led to the belief that many of his claims were untrue and, by 1953, he was discredited – although by then the Rosenbergs had been executed.
- Despite becoming full US citizens in 1866, by 1945 African-Americans still experienced racist discrimination and even violence – especially in the Southern states of the USA, where Jim Crow laws existed.
- Civil rights organisations (such as the NAACP and CORE) began to campaign for equal rights and the end of segregation in what some referred to as the 'Freedom Movement'.
- Despite being encouraged to take jobs during the Second World War to help the war effort, women were encouraged to return to the home and women's 'traditional' roles. Those who stayed in employment experienced unequal pay and promotion prospects.

1954–62

- The early civil rights groups believed in peaceful protest and non-violent direct action. An early success was the Montgomery Bus Boycott in 1955–6, intended to end segregation on public transport. One of the leaders who emerged from that campaign was Martin Luther King.
- Another campaign was waged against segregation in education (Brown vs. Board of Education) – despite a Supreme Court ruling in 1954 that it was illegal, no date was set for introducing integration.
- In 1957, efforts to end segregation in schools then centred on Little Rock Central High School, Arkansas – violent protests by white mobs forced President Eisenhower to send federal troops to allow black students to enter the school. Similar events took place in 1962 in order to allow James Meredith to enrol at the University of Missisippi.

Section 8: The USA, 1945–75 continued•

Other protests in 1960–1 were over segregation in restaurants, with Freedom Riders also checking on desegregation of bus station facilities.

1963–8

- In 1963, the Civil Rights Movement waged a big desegregation campaign in Birmingham, Alabama. There was much violence from white police and racists – President Kennedy was forced to send in federal troops.
- As Congress began to consider a Civil Rights Bill, the Civil Rights Movement organised the massive March on Washington. In 1964, following more violent opposition to civil rights campaigners in Missisippi, the Civil Rights Act was finally passed.
- However, many problems continued (e.g. police violence) and the increasing violence experienced by civil rights campaigners led some to consider that Martin Luther King's peaceful methods were ineffective – they called for more radical and even violent responses.
- Such individuals and groups included Malcolm X, Stokely Carmichael, Black Power and the Black Panthers. Riots broke out in 1965–7, and the violence increased when Martin Luther King was assassinated in 1968.
- In 1963, Betty Freidan's *The Feminine Mystique* sparked off a new feminist movement and, in 1966, NOW was set up. Soon, radical feminist and Women's Liberation groups were set up all over the USA, and women campaigned for equal civil rights in education and employment.
- The 1960s also saw student protests against US foreign policy – especially the war in Vietnam – and against poverty, intolerance and white racism in the USA. Particularly important for a time was the Students for a Democratic Society (SDS) organisation.
- While many young people decided to 'drop out' during the 1960s, the SDS organised demonstrations and the public burning of draft cards of those called up to fight in Vietnam.

1969–75

- Despite Martin Luther King's assassination, some African-Americans began to get elected to positions of power, and the end of segregation in education allowed many to get better qualifications and jobs. This continued to improve during the early 1970s, despite continuing problems of poverty, poor housing and public services for many blacks.
- Other ethnic minorities also campaigned for equal rights during this period – such as Native Americans and Hispanic-Americans. In addition, during the 1960s and 1970s, there were important women's liberation and student protest movements.
- While most student protests were peaceful, some became violent – in 1970, at Kent State University, National Guard troops were called in to deal with a students' strike and sit-in against the US invasion of Cambodia – four protesters were shot dead. During the early 1970s, the SDS began to break up.

Section 9: Britain, 1900–14

1900–5

- By 1900, Britain had the largest empire in the world, but many staple industries faced increased competition and there was much poverty.
- The Conservatives, who had dominated British politics since 1886, were forced to resign in 1905.

1906–9

- In the January 1906 elections, the Liberals won a massive majority.
- The new Liberal government immediately began a huge reform programme.
- In 1909, Lloyd George (the Chancellor of the Exchequer) introduced the Old Age Pensions Act.

1909–11

- These reforms, and especially old-age pensions, needed extra taxation to pay for them. Lloyd George introduced the 'People's Budget' in 1909, which increased taxes on the wealthy.
- The Budget was blocked by the House of Lords.
- After two elections in 1910 (won by the Liberals), the Parliament Act of 1911 reduced the powers of the Lords, and the Budget was passed.
- The Liberals also faced other problems: the Suffragette campaign for votes for women; and the question of Home Rule in Ireland.

1911–14

- Although these problems worsened after 1911, the Liberals continued with their reforms.
- After 1911, the Labour Party began to rival the Liberals, causing many Liberals to adopt New Liberalism.
- This led to several reforms, especially the National Insurance Act, 1911.
- Industrial conflict also increased, with the three main unions forming the Triple Industrial Alliance (TIA).
- But all problems were put on hold when the First World War began in 1914.

Section 10: Britain, 1914–18

1914–16

- When Britain declared war on Germany, thousands rushed to volunteer. But, in 1916, conscription was introduced.
- Some men were exempted from conscription: the medically unfit, and those in 'essential' war jobs.
- However, there were also about 16 000 conscientious objectors.
- Because the First World War was the first 'total' war, the home front became important. In 1914, DORA was rushed through Parliament to give emergency powers to the government.
- In particular, it allowed the government to take over any factory for war production.
- The War Propaganda Bureau drew up false stories about the Germans, and bad news was suppressed.
- Civilians became targets of German ships and Zeppelins in an attempt to break civilian morale.
- But Britain took effective steps to counter the Zeppelins.

1917–18

- So, in 1917, the Germans switched to Gotha IV bomber planes.
- Also, by the end of 1916, the German U-boat campaign was causing serious food shortages in Britain.
- In 1917, the government introduced voluntary rationing.
- But this failed and the German U-boat campaign was stepped up. So, in 1918, rationing became compulsory.
- With so many men at the front, serious labour shortages arose – these gaps were filled by women.
- Many women worked in munitions factories, engineering factories, or became conductors on trams and buses.
- Many joined the Women's Land Army, the VADs, FANY, or one of the women's military units.
- In 1918, women over the age of 30 were, at last, given the vote.

Section 11: Britain, 1918–39

1918–22

- After the war, there was a short depression.
- This led to a rise in industrial disputes and the revival of the TIA, as employers wanted to cut wages. Problems were worst in the mining industry.
- There was also trouble in Ireland, following the Easter Rebellion of 1916. When Sinn Fein won the majority of Irish seats in 1918, a war of independence broke out. Eventually, in 1922, Ireland was partitioned.

1923–9

- The Conservatives came to power in 1923. Problems in the mining industry worsened.
- In 1925, the government gave a subsidy to mine owners to prevent wage cuts, after the TIA threatened strike action. But it also set up the OMS to prepare for a General Strike.
- The TUC called a general strike in May 1926, but it was called off after nine days.

1929–31

- In 1929, Labour won the election but, after the US Wall Street Crash in 1929, the Depression soon caused high unemployment in Britain.
- Labour ministers disagreed over what action to take, and MacDonald resigned.

1931–9

- The King asked MacDonald to form a coalition National Government with the Conservatives.
- Unemployment rose, and a means test was introduced for those claiming the 'dole'.
- There were 'hunger marches' in protest – the most famous was the Jarrow Crusade in 1936.
- By 1937, the National Government was really a Conservative government in all but name.

Section 12: Britain, 1939–45

1939–40

- In 1937–38, before the war began, the government had recruited ARP wardens and introduced limited conscription. In 1939, all males aged 19 to 41 were conscripted; later, the minimum age was reduced to 18.
- After Dunkirk, the Local Defence Volunteers was set up – they were soon renamed as the Home Guard.
- A Schedule of Reserved Occupations was drawn up to defer the conscription of specialist workers.
- The government also took extra powers under the Emergency Powers Act, 1939. Most industry was quickly placed under government control
- Over 1.5 million children were evacuated from the major cities, and people were provided with bomb shelters.
- After the Battle of Britain, the Blitz began as German planes bombed industrial and civilian areas in major cities.
- Because of German U-boat attacks, rationing was introduced in 1940.

1941–3

- Because so many men were in the armed forces, all single women aged 19 to 30 were conscripted. They could join one of the women's sections in the armed forces, organisations such as the ATS or the ATA, or work in factories or on the land.
- During 1942–43, air raids continued, but were less heavy and often on less well-defended towns and cities.
- As the Allies began to win the Battle of the Atlantic, the food situation became less serious.

1944–5

- In 1944 and 1945, British cities were attacked by V1 flying bombs and V2 rockets. Between them, these new weapons killed or injured approximately 30 000 civilians.

Section 13: Britain, 1945–79

1945–9

- In July 1945, the Labour Party won a massive victory in the general election – in part, because it was committed to introducing the welfare reforms suggested by the Beveridge Report in 1942.
- Its biggest social reform was the setting up of the National Health Service – an entirely free health service. Despite much opposition from many doctors who feared losing income from private medicine, this reform was pushed through by Aneurin Bevan in 1948.
- As well as other social welfare reforms, the new Labour government also nationalised several essential industries, some of which were on the point of collapse (e.g. the railways and coal industry).
- After the Second World War, the British economy was slow to recover, with rationing continuing for several years.
- As Britain's economy declined after the Second World War, so did its position as a world power.
- Many former colonies – often after bitter nationalist struggles – won their independence from Britain, beginning with India in 1947.
- After the Second World War, the need to rebuild the country and the economy meant that many women were encouraged by the government to stay in employment.
- However, most women experienced inequalities as regards pay and promotion – and tended to be found mainly in jobs linked to traditional women's roles in the home.

1950–9

- The Conservatives won the election in 1951 – despite their earlier opposition to nationalisation, they only returned steel to the former private owners.
- After the Second World War, there was much reconstruction to do in Britain, while the new NHS and other welfare services were also being introduced – but had insufficient numbers of workers.
- To overcome this, British governments encouraged people from the Commonweath (e.g. the West Indies, India, Pakistan) to come to Britain to work and settle.
- However, this was opposed by some white people.
- From the mid-1950s, affluence increased, leading to a boom in consumer spending.
- But there were serious underlying economic problems – the lack of investment by companies in new technology, a falling share of world trade and a growing balance of payments deficit.
- In addition, rising inflation led to problems with industrial relations as trade unions tried to protect their members' real wages and jobs.
- Overseas, decolonisation spread to Africa during the 1960s. An attempt to retain a world role in 1956 led to the Suez fiasco.
- These developments led some British politicians to turn increasingly to Europe – in particular, towards the EEC.
- During the 1950s, women benefited from the various welfare reforms introduced by Labour before 1951, such as the NHS, while increased affluence allowed the purchase of labour-saving domestic appliances.
- Many more women began to want to resume their careers once their children had reached school age.

1960–9

- In 1968, leading Conservative Enoch Powell made his infamous 'Rivers of Blood' speech in response to immigration.
- During this period, a number of immigration and race relations acts were passed.
- Far-right groups, such as the National Front and, later, the BNP, began to exploit these racial tensions by organising protests, which were often violent.
- In Northern Ireland, the inequalities and discrimination experienced by Catholics at the hands of Protestant employers and the Protestant-dominated government at Stormont triggered protests that led to the Northern Ireland Civil Rights Association (NICRA) being set up in 1967.
- NICRA marches were met by violent Protestant mobs – and the B Special police often joined these mobs in attacking the protesters.
- These clashes led to the revival of the IRA and increased violence – in 1969, the British government sent in troops to keep the peace. But the violence only increased.
- During this period, increasing affluence led to an explosion of different youth cultures and styles, and to an increasingly radical student movement from the mid-1960s – the latter demonstrating against issues such as nuclear weapons, the war in Vietnam, apartheid in South Africa and the emerging fascist/far-right groups.
- Attempts by both Conservative and Labour governments to deal with Britain's economic problems by controlling wage increases and increasing productivity led to more tensions – and attempts to restrict trade union rights.
- Many British politicians were more concerned to maintain the special relationship with the USA – which wanted Britain to play a supporting role in the Cold War. But, as Britain began to decline, it became increasingly dependent on the USA (e.g. in 1960, Britain's independent nuclear deterrent relied on US missiles and warheads).
- The increased costs of maintaining a presence 'East of Suez' eventually led Britain to close most of its foreign military bases – despite objections from the USA.
- Early attempts to join the EEC in the 1960s were blocked by France, which distrusted Britain's closeness to the USA.
- During the 1960s, the continuing discrimination and inequalities in employment and pay led to the rise of feminist groups and campaigns for equal opportunities in education.
- From the late 1960s, a women's liberation movement began to develop, inspired by such writers as Germaine Greer. Soon, most major towns had a Women's Liberation group. Their campaigns resulted in various reforms from1967–70 (including Labour's Equal Pay Act and Employment Protection Act, both passed in 1969).

1970–9

- In 1971, internment was introduced in Northern Ireland – a protest against this in January 1972 led to the incident known as 'Bloody Sunday', when British paratroopers shot dead thirteen protesters.
- Stormont was abolished and Direct Rule from Westminster introduced – but the violence continued to escalate. The IRA split, and the new Provisional IRA began to carry out terrorist attacks in mainland Britain.
- The Conservatives' Industrial Relations Act 1972 led to widespread opposition from unions and a number of strikes. These problems continued under the new 1974–9 Labour government.
- In 1973, Britain became a member of the EEC – this was confirmed by a referendum in 1975.
- In 1970, a national conference of such groups agreed on four main demands. Continuing campaigns led to further reforms (such as Labour's Sex Discrimination Act, 1975) – as the 1970s closed, new issues came to the fore, such as sexual exploitation, violence towards women (especially domestic violence) and sexual harassment at work.

Notes

Acknowledgements

© Bettmann/CORBIS (British dreadnought, HMS *Barham*), **p. 3**; Getty Images (Franz Ferdinand and wife), **p. 5**; Peter Newark's Pictures (Berliners scavenging for food, 1918), **p. 11**; Getty Images (Lloyd George, Clemenceau and Wilson in Paris, 1919), **p. 13**; News International Ltd ('Treaty of Versilles' cartoon, *The Daily Herald*, 10 December 1919), **p. 15**; e.t. archive (French World War I poster), **p. 17**, The Punch Cartoon Library ('The gap in the bridge' cartoon), **p. 19**; Solo Syndication ('Trial by Geneva' cartoon, *Evening Standard*, 1931), **p. 23**; David King Collection, London ('The Munich Agreement' cartoon), **p. 35**; akg-images (boycott of Jewish shops, 1933), **p. 47**; Getty Images (American family, 1920s), **p. 49**; Getty Images (Sunderland slum), **p. 91**; Mary Evans Picture Library (WSPU poster), **p. 93**; Getty Images ('The dawn of hope' government poster, 1911), **p. 95**; Getty Images (female bus conductor, London, 1917), **p. 101**; Hulton-Deutsch Collection/CORBIS (Black and Tan soldiers), **p. 105**; Getty Images (Home Guards), **p. 109**; Getty Images (Anderson shelters), **p. 111**; Getty Images (Women's Land Army) **p. 113 (left)**; Imperial War Museum (SOE agents), **p. 113 (right)**; The Punch Cartoon Library ('Dotheboys Hall' cartoon, *Punch*, 1948), **p.115**; Getty Images (Grunswick dispute), **p. 119 (top)**; Wally Fawkes (Trog) ('Tropy heads' cartoon, the *Observer*, April 1979), **p. 119 (bottom)**; Rex Features (abortion demonstration, 1973), **p. 127 (left)**; Getty Images (marriage demonstration), **p. 127 (right)**; Getty Images (Soviet partisan fighters), **p. 134**; Bettmann/CORBIS (Elizabeth Eckford), **p. 136**; Advertising Archives (government poster), **138 (left)**; Alamy (Women's Land Army harvesting oats, 1941), **p. 138 (right)**

Every effort has been made to trace the copyright holders of the material used in this resource. In instances where we may have failed to do so, we would be happy to rectify this at the first available opportunity.